restaurants in california

Restaurants in California

Edited by Gen Takeshi Saito©

First published in 1993 by
Graphic-sha Publishing Co., Ltd.
1-9-12, Kudan-kita, Chiyoda-ku, Tokyo 102 Japan
Phone: 81-3-3263-4318
Fax: 81-3-3263-5297

All rights reserved. No part of this publication may be reproduced
or used in any form or by any means — graphic, electronic, or
mechanical, including photocopying, recording, taping, or
information storage and retrieval systems — without written permission
of the publisher.

Printed in Japan by Toppan Printing Co., Ltd.

ISBM 4-7661-0748-9 C2052

カリフォルニア レストラン

FOREWORD

After a long period of recession, the world economy is still sluggish, and signs of recovery are quite vague. In these circumstances, the American restaurant industry is no exception, and, at the risk of "survival," restaurants are groping for a way out while repeating trials and errors through new construction, extension or renovation, or changes in menu composition, prices, etc. Thus, all aspects of management are being reviewed and changed.

As for dishes, the mainstream is shifting from gourmet oriented items to more health oriented items cooked by directly utilizing fresh ingredients. As for shop making, the types of interior and operation are changing to those which are more conscious of environment and comfort to satisfy customers, and may be said to be inclined towards casualness.

This book contains 51 restaurants which have opened in cities in California including Los Angeles, Santa Monica and San Francisco, and are operating successfully due to unique concepts which are hotly talked about and gaining popularity. They include the sister shops of "REMI," "PLANET HOLLYWOOD," "LUMA," etc. which have succeeded in New York on the East Coast, as well as "LULU," "OPUS," etc. which were recently opened by the owners of those East Coast restaurants. Their design may be generally said to have taken root as bright, open and casual "Californian style" in harmony with the environment.

As for types of operation, in addition to Italian and French restaurants, ethnic and specialty restaurants have gained popularity. By utilizing fresh and abundant ingredients available in California, they are developing new types of foods which are served at lower prices.

This book introduces the shop interiors and plans, as well as the menu design used at each restaurant, crew uniforms, dishes recommended by the chef (dish names are given in the original language), etc.

I would be more than pleased if, through this book, readers can feel what restaurants are like "now," and refer to the contents when making or operating a shop. Many thanks go to the restaurants which kindly cooperated with me in collecting data, and to Mrs. Barbara M. Dawson, a restaurant consultant and journalist living in Los Angeles, and one of my friends of long standing. I also express my hearty thanks to Mr. Hiroshi Tsujita of Graphic-sha Publishing Co., Ltd., who has undertaken the editing, as well as to other persons concerned.

September 1993
Gen Takeshi Saito

はじめに

世界的な経済不況と言われてから長く いまだに停滞し続け その脱出の兆しさえおぼろげの状態である。 このような時代にあって アメリカの外食産業界においても例外でなく 今や"生き残り"をかけ 模索と試行錯誤を繰り返し 店舗の新築 増改築 メニュー構成や価格などあらゆる分野で見直しが行われ 変化が現れている。

料理では かつての高級志向から 本質の追求こそ変わらないが より健康を考慮したもので素材を活かしたものに移ってきている。店づくりにおいては 環境や快適さを考慮した利用客サイドにあわせたインテリアや業態に変わってきており よりカジュアル化の傾向にあるといえよう。

本書には そのような動きのあるこの数年の間に ロサンゼルスをはじめ サンタモニカ サンフランシスコなど カリフォルニアに誕生し ユニークなコンセプトで話題や人気を集め成功しているレストラン 51店を収録している。これらの店のなかには よく比較対象となる東海岸のニューヨークで成功をおさめた「REMI」や「PLANET HOLLYWOOD」「LUMA」などの進出や それらのオーナーたちが新たにオープンさせた「LULU」「OPUS」なども含まれ デザイン的には 環境にあわせ 明るく開放的で カジュアルな"カリフォルニアスタイル"として定着したといえよう。

業種としてはイタリアン フレンチのほかに エスニックやスペシャリティレストランがポピュラー化し カリフォルニアの新鮮で豊富な食材と相まって新しい発想の料理の開発 メニュー構成 低価格化などに工夫が感じられる。

本書では 店舗のインテリアや平面プランに加え 各レストランが使用しているメニューブックのデザインやユニフォーム シェフの薦める料理(料理名は原文のまま)などを紹介している。

本書を通して"いま"のレストランの動きを感じ 店づくり 運営の参考にしていただければ幸いである。取材にあたり ご協力いただいた掲載店 そして 永年の友人 ロサンゼルス在住のレストラン コンサルタントでジャーナリストの Mrs,Barbara M.Dawson 出版にあたり グラフィック社の編集担当 辻田 博氏 ほか関係各位に深く感謝します。

1993年 9月　斎藤　武

(Gen Takeshi Saito)

Contents

PLANET HOLLYWOOD ⟨Santa Ana⟩ 10

CAFE DEL RAY ⟨Marina Del Ray⟩ 15

HARD ROCK CAFE ⟨Newport Beach⟩ 20

CHA CHA CHA Encino ⟨Encino⟩ 24

CHA CHA CHA Long Beach ⟨Long Beach⟩ 29

BORDER GRILL ⟨Santa Monica⟩ 34

CYPRESS CLUB ⟨San Francisco⟩ 38

CAFE LA BOHEME ⟨West Hollywood⟩ 42

SCHATZI ON MAIN ⟨Santa Monica⟩ 46

BAYSIDE 240 ⟨Redondo Beach⟩ 50

RED CAR GRILL ⟨West Hollywood⟩ 54

BLACKHAWK GRILL ⟨Danville⟩ 58

RESTAURANT LULU ⟨San Francisco⟩ 62

TERRAZZA TOSCANA ⟨Encino⟩ 66

McCORMICK & KULETO'S SEAFOOD RESTAURANT ⟨San Francisco⟩ 70

ETRUSCA ⟨San Francisco⟩ 74

I CUGINI TRATTORIA ⟨Santa Monica⟩ 78

IL FORNAIO CUCINA EXPRESSA ⟨Costa Mesa⟩ 82

BROADWAY DELI ⟨Santa Monica⟩ 86

CALIFORNIA BEACH ROCK N' SUSHI ⟨Los Angeles⟩ 90

THE STINKING ROSE ⟨San Francisco⟩ 94

CAFE VALLARTA ⟨Santa Barbara⟩ 98

FAMA ⟨Santa Monica⟩ 102

REMI ⟨Santa Monica⟩ 106

MISS PEARL'S JAM HOUSE ⟨San Francisco⟩ 110

DALE'S BISTRO ⟨Los Angeles⟩ 114

CIMARRON ⟨Beverly Hills⟩ 118

GORDON BIERSCH ⟨San Francisco⟩ 122

CHILLERS ⟨Santa Monica⟩ 126

PARAGON BAR & CAFE ⟨San Francisco⟩ 130

JOHNNY LOVE'S ⟨San Francisco⟩ 134

LAWRY'S THE PRIME RIB ⟨Beverly Hills⟩ 138

LUNARIA ⟨Los Angeles⟩ 142

RÖKENWAGNER ⟨Santa Monica⟩ 146

MICHAEL'S WATERSIDE ⟨Santa Barbara⟩ 150

AQUA ⟨San Francisco⟩ 154

ONE MARKET RESTAURANT ⟨San Francisco⟩ 158

ELKA ⟨San Francisco⟩ 162

WATER GRILL ⟨Los Angeles⟩ 166

NORTH BEACH BAR & GRILL ⟨Venice⟩ 170

L'OPERA RISTORANTE ⟨Long Beach⟩ 174

BIKINI ⟨Santa Monica⟩ 178

OPUS RESTAURANT ⟨Santa Monica⟩ 182

PINOT BISTRO ⟨Studio City⟩ 186

EMPORIO ARMANI EXPRESS ⟨Costa Mesa⟩ 191

L'ESCOFFIER ⟨Beverly Hills⟩ 194

PICNIC ⟨Los Angeles⟩ 197

TATOU ⟨Beverly Hills⟩ 200

LUMA ⟨Santa Monica⟩ 203

POST ⟨Sherman Oaks⟩ 208

MODELLA RISTORANTE ⟨San Francisco⟩ 212

Index 217

目次

プラネット ハリウッド〈サンタ アナ〉10
カフェ デル レイ〈マリーナ デル レイ〉15
ハードロック カフェ〈ニューポートビーチ〉20
チャ チャ チャ エンシノ店〈エンシノ〉24
チャ チャ チャ ロングビーチ店〈ロングビーチ〉29
ボーダー グリル〈サンタモニカ〉34
サイプレス クラブ〈サンフランシスコ〉38
カフェ ラ ボエム〈ウエスト ハリウッド〉42
シャッツィ オン メイン〈サンタモニカ〉46
ベイサイド 240〈レドンドビーチ〉50
レッドカー グリル〈ウエスト ハリウッド〉54
ブラックホーク グリル〈ダンヴィル〉58
レストラン ルル〈サンフランシスコ〉62
テラッツァ トスカーナ〈エンシノ〉66
マッコーミック＆クレートズ シーフードレストラン
〈サンフランシスコ〉70
エトラスカ〈サンフランシスコ〉74
イ クジーニ トラットリア〈サンタモニカ〉78
イル フォナイオ クチーナ エキスプレッサ
〈コスタ メサ〉82
ブロードウェイ デリ〈サンタモニカ〉86
カリフォルニアビーチ ロックン スシ〈ロサンゼルス〉90
ザ スティンキング ローズ〈サンフランシスコ〉94
カフェ バヤルタ〈サンタバーバラ〉98
ファーマ〈サンタモニカ〉102
レミ〈サンタモニカ〉106
ミス パールス ジャム ハウス〈サンフランシスコ〉110
デイルズ ビストロ〈ロサンゼルス〉114

シマロン〈ビバリーヒルズ〉118
ゴードン ビアーシュ〈サンフランシスコ〉122
チラーズ〈サンタモニカ〉126
パラゴン バー＆カフェ〈サンフランシスコ〉130
ジョニー ラブス〈サンフランシスコ〉134
ローリース ザ プライム リブ〈ビバリーヒルズ〉138
ルナーリア〈ロサンゼルス〉142
レッケンバグナー〈サンタモニカ〉146
マイケルズ ウォーターサイド〈サンタバーバラ〉150
アクア〈サンフランシスコ〉154
ワン マーケット レストラン〈サンフランシスコ〉158
エルカ〈サンフランシスコ〉162
ウォーター グリル〈ロサンゼルス〉166
ノースビーチ バー＆グリル〈ベニス〉170
ル オペラ リストランテ〈ロングビーチ〉174
ビキニ〈サンタモニカ〉178
オプス レストラン〈サンタモニカ〉182
ピノ ビストロ〈スタジオ シティ〉186
エンポリオ アルマーニ エキスプレス〈コスタ メサ〉191
エスコフィエ〈ビバリーヒルズ〉194
ピクニック〈ロサンゼルス〉197
タトー〈ビバリーヒルズ〉200
ルマ〈サンタモニカ〉203
ポスト〈シャーマンオークス〉208
モデラ リストランテ〈サンフランシスコ〉212

索引 217

PLANET HOLLYWOOD
⟨Santa Ana⟩

An entertainment restaurant featuring the world of the movies and TV as a motif. This restaurant, opened after the opening of a chain restaurant in New York, is situated near a shopping center on the South Coast Plaza which houses many first-class shops. It is hotly talked about because VIPs in the film world such as Bo Derek, an actress and film producer, Arnold Schwarzenegger, and Sylvester Stallone, are involved in its management. In the restaurant, costumes and props used by them in the movies are displayed so that guests can enjoy eating while recalling various scenes. It also serves as a pleasant place for movie fans to communicate with movie stars. It serves new-wave Californian classic cuisine, and offers fast-selling character goods at a retail corner.
<PLANET HOLLYWOOD>
Number of guest seats/263
Address/1641 West Sunflower Santa Ana, CA 92704
Phone/714-434-7827   Fax/714-957-9311

映画とテレビの世界をモチーフにしたエンターテイメント レストラン。ニューヨークに続き出店したこのレストランは 高級店が集まるサウスコーストプラザのショッピングセンターの近くに立地している。
女優で映画製作者のボー デレック（Bo Derek）を中心に アーノルド シュワルツェネッガー（Arnold Schwarzenegger）や シルベスター スターン（Sylvester Stallone）など 大物の映画関係者が経営陣に名を連ね話題になっている。店づくりのコンセプトは彼らが映画で使用した衣装や小道具がディスプレイされ 訪れた人たちが映画の場面を想い出しながら 食事を楽しむといったところにあり スターとの交流などで映画ファンを喜ばせている。カリフォルニアの新しいクラシック料理を提供し 売店コーナーではキャラクター商品を扱い売上をのばしている。
〈プラネット ハリウッド〉
客席数/263席
Address/1641 West Sunflower Santa Ana, CA 92704
Phone/714-434-7827   Fax/714-957-9311

①

②

③

④

1/The wall on which a night scene of Hollywood is presented; colors and atmosphere are changed by lighting.
2/The central part of the interior; with an open kitchen (left) and dining room.
3/The uniform is colorful.
4/The bar area; installed in a stairwell. On the wall, props and costumes used in the movies are displayed and spotlighted.
5/The facade.

1/ハリウッドの夜景を演出した壁面　照明で色や雰囲気を変化させている
2/店内中央部　オープンキッチン(左)とダイニングをみる
3/ユニフォームはカラフル
4/バーエリア　吹き抜けになっており　壁面には映画で使用された小道具や衣類がディスプレイされ スポットライトがあてられている
5/ファサード

⑤

6/Schwarzenegger's rotating cyborg model.
7/The 2nd floor; the dining room, which features a full bar.
8/Smoking is permitted only on the 2nd floor; a film is continuously shown on the large 12×10 inch screen.
9/The spotlighted tabletop and props displayed on the wall.

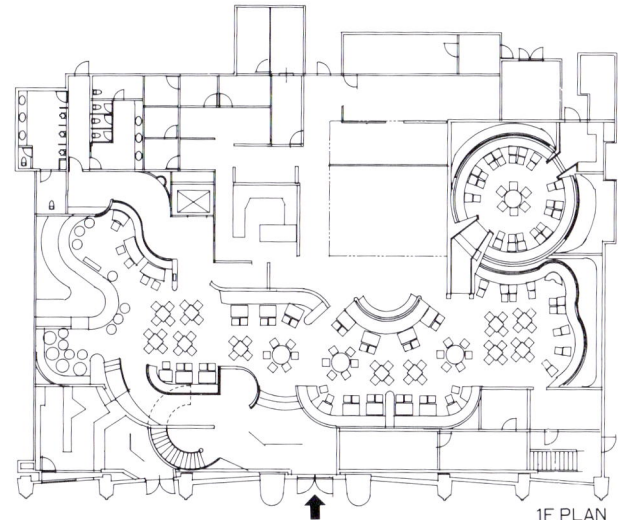

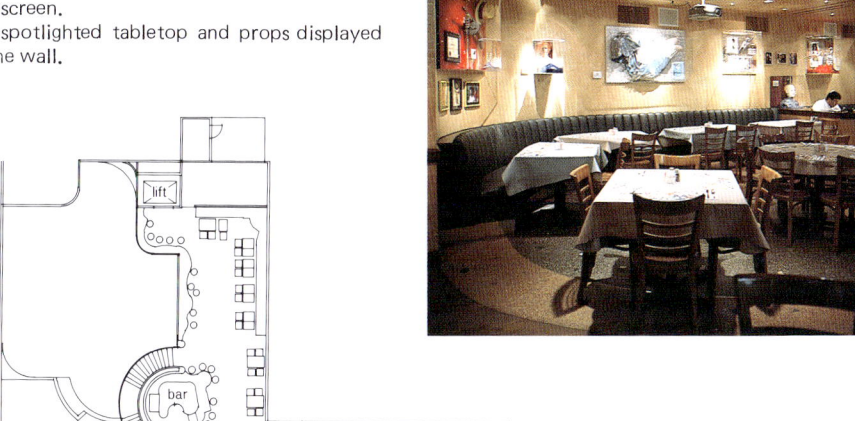

2F PLAN

1F PLAN

6/シュワルツェネッガーのサイボーグの模型が回転する
7/2階 フルバーのあるダイニングルーム
8/2階のみ喫煙が可能 12×10インチの大型スクリーンを設け 常時映画を上映している
9/スポットライトに照らされたテーブルトップと壁面にディスプレイされた小道具類

● menu
a : RANCH PORK CHOPS/Tow marinated center-cut pork chops 6 oz. each, grilled to order.
b : BLACKENED CHICKEN BREAST/Chicken breast blackened and served on an onion turnover with creole mustard, lettuce tomato and red onions.
c : PISA PIZZA/A red sauce base, with julienned cappicola, Italian sausage, black olives, fresh tomatoes and topped with Mozzarella and Parmesan cheese.
d : EBONY AND IVORY BROWNIE/A layered white and dark chocolate ice creams and chocolate and caramel sauces. Finished with whipped cream and chopped nuts.

CAFE DEL RAY
⟨Marina Del Ray⟩

A restaurant favorably situated in Marina Del Ray which is known as a yacht harbor, and facing the sea. It is operated by the California Cafe Restaurant Corp. which is developing the "California Cafe" restaurant chain centering around San Francisco. It has advanced into Los Angeles for the first time.

"Cafe Del Ray" serves new-style dishes by combining Pacific coastal foods with traditional French foods centering around Mediterranean cuisine. These foods cooked by a Japanese chef are quite original and their presentation is also highly rated. From the contemporary interior space, guests can look at the yacht harbor. Thus, the restaurant is hotly discussed by those who come to enjoy boating or cycling, as well as by neighboring inhabitants and visitors.

⟨CAFE DEL RAY⟩
Number of guest seats/190 (restaurant 140, bar 50)
Address/4451 Admiralty Way Marina Del Ray, CA 90292
Phone/213-823-6395

ヨットハーバーとして知られるマリーナ デル レイ地区の海に面した好立地のレストラン。経営はサンフランシスコを中心に「カリフォルニア カフェ」レストランチェーンを展開する California Cafe restaurant Corp.でロサンゼルス地域へは初めての進出である。料理は地中海地方を中心に伝統的なフランス料理と太平洋地域の料理を組合わせた新しいスタイルのもので 日本人シェフが作る料理は独創的で その盛り付け(プレゼンテーション)も評価が高い。コンテンポラリーな明るい店内からはヨットハーバーが眺められ ボートやサイクリングを楽しむ人たち 近くの住人やビジターの間で評判のレストランになっている。

⟨カフェ デル レイ⟩
客席数/190席(レストラン 140席 バー 50席)
Address/4451 Admiralty Way Marina Del Ray, CA 90292
Phone/213-823-6395

1・2/The restaurant facing the yacht harbor; with a logo on the facade.

1・2/ヨットハーバーに面したレストラン 正面にロゴを配している

③

④

⑤

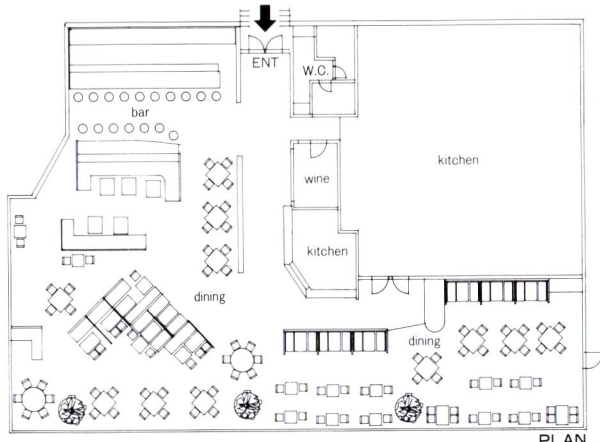

PLAN

3/The dining room has an open atmosphere.
4/The bar counter.
5/The lounge.
6/The open kitchen in the center of the restaurant.

3/開放的なダイニングルーム
4/バーカウンターをみる
5/ラウンジ
6/レストランの中央部にあるオープンキッチン

(a)

(b)

(d)

(c)

●menu
a : Sashimi Salad with Crispy Noodles, Spaghetti Cucumber and Yuzu Dressing.
b : Crab Cakes, Pink Grapefruit Sauce, Mache and Fried Leeks.
c : Oven Roasted Halibut with Shrimps, Scallops, Fried Okura and Tamari Curry.
d : Housemade Assortment of Fruit Sorbets, Almond Tuile and Cookies.

7/The dining room whose upper part is partitioned by trass; the wall is decorated with founded pieces of art.

7/上部をトラスで仕切られたダイニング 壁面にはファウンド アートが飾られている。

⑦

HARD ROCK CAFE
⟨Newport Beach⟩

Opened at the end of 1992 on a favorable location adjoining the Fashion Island Shopping Center, this is the latest shop of the "Hard Rock Cafe" chain which has been hotly accepted by young people for its unique interior composition based on rock 'n' roll as a theme and casual American foods. Since the first shop in the U.K. opened in 1971 and the first Los Angeles shop in the U.S.A. opened in 1982, direct-run and franchise shops have been successfully operated and there are 18 cafes at present. They are yearly visited by a total of 750,000 guests and 60% of them are said to be tourists.

In the shop, rock is aired and photos of famous rock singers are displayed on the wall, thus creating an atmosphere like a museum. Mr. Peter Morton, one of the founders, said that they wished to make a shop where people loving rock can enjoy popular American foods at reasonable prices. Meanwhile, through a campaign called "Save the Planet," they have sponsored many charity activities, thus advancing concern about social and environmental problems.

⟨HARD ROCK CAFE⟩
Number of guest seats/260
Address/451 Newport Center Drive Newport Beach, CA
Phone/714-640-8844

ロックンロールをテーマにしたユニークな店内構成とカジュアルなアメリカ料理で若者たちに人気の「ハードロック カフェ」の最新店で '92年暮 ファッションアイランド ショッピングセンターに隣接した好立地にオープンした。'71年 イギリスのロンドンに1号店 '82年にロサンゼルスにアメリカの1号店を出店以来 多くのロックファンたちなどに親しまれ現在 直営店とフランチャイズ店を合わせ 18店舗を展開している。年間で合計75万人の客が訪れ そのうち60%がツーリストだという。

店内にはロックが流れ 壁面には有名ロック歌手のコレクションが飾られミュージアムを思わせる雰囲気である。創始者の一人 ピーター モートン(Peter Morton)は "ロックを愛し アメリカ人たちが親しんでいる料理を リーズナブルな価格で楽しめる" 店づくりをモットーにしたという。一方で "セイブ ザ プラネット"というキャンペーンで 多くのチャリティ事業を催し 人間や環境問題にも取り組んでいる。

⟨ハードロック カフェ⟩
客席数/260席
Address/451 Newport Center Drive Newport Beach, CA
Phone/714-640-8844

1/The signboard — the world's largest (40 feet) electric guitar.
2/The facade; adjoining the shopping center.
3/The dining room with a '59 Cadillac named "Play for Surf."

1/サインボード 40フィートもある世界最大のエレキギター
2/ファサード ショッピングセンターに隣接している
3/ "Play for Surf"と名付けられた'59年型のキャデラックがあるダイニング

NEWPORT BEACH
Hard Rock
CAFE

④

⑤

ENT
reception
kitchen
bar
office

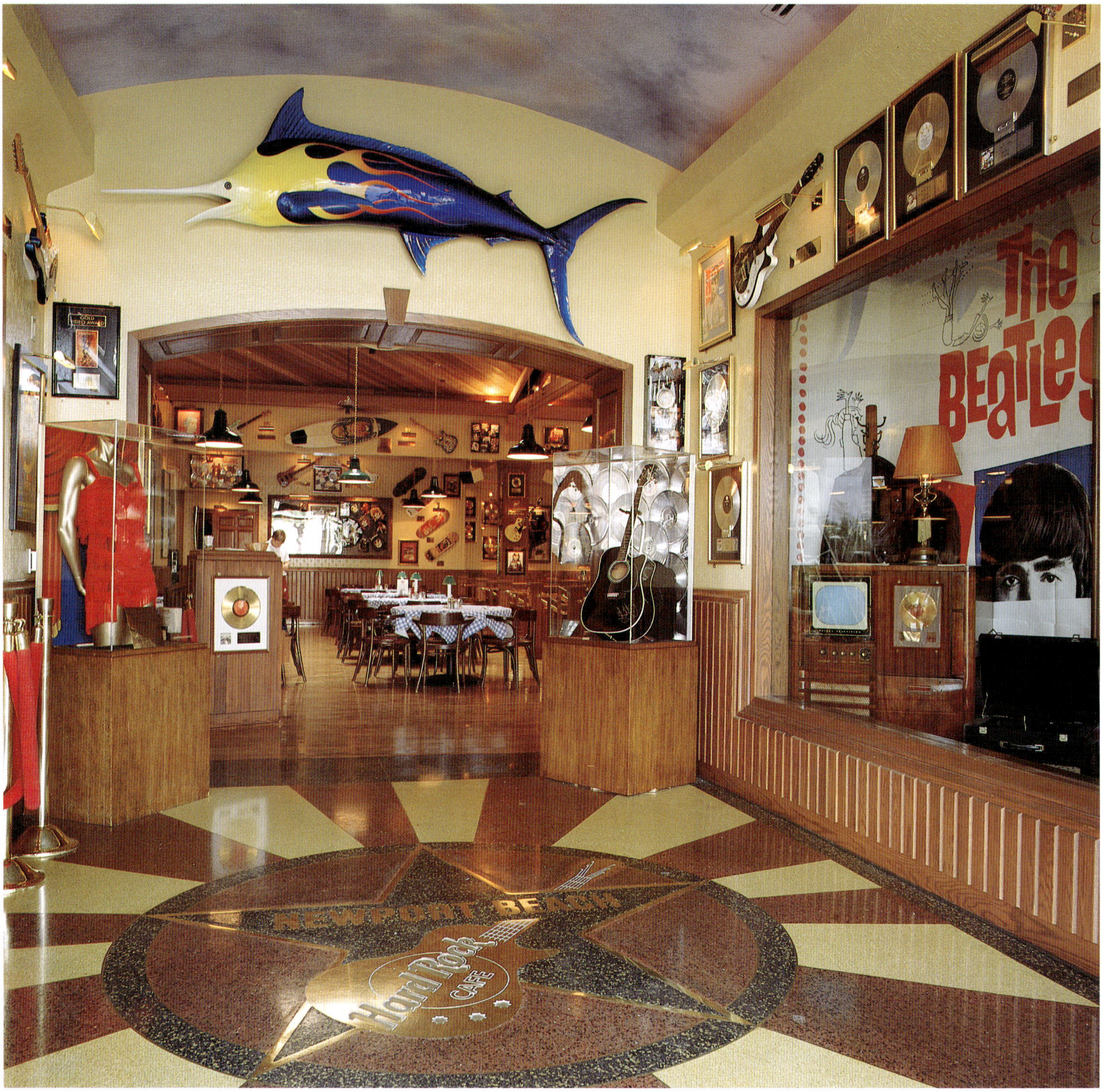

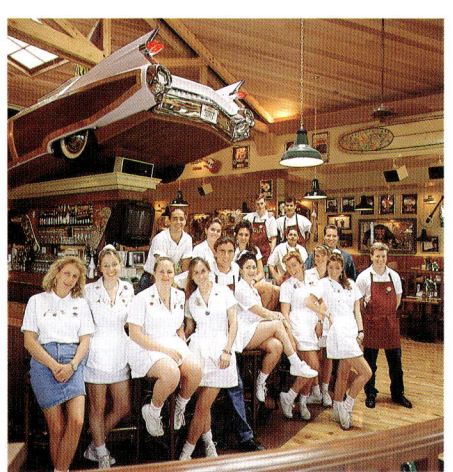

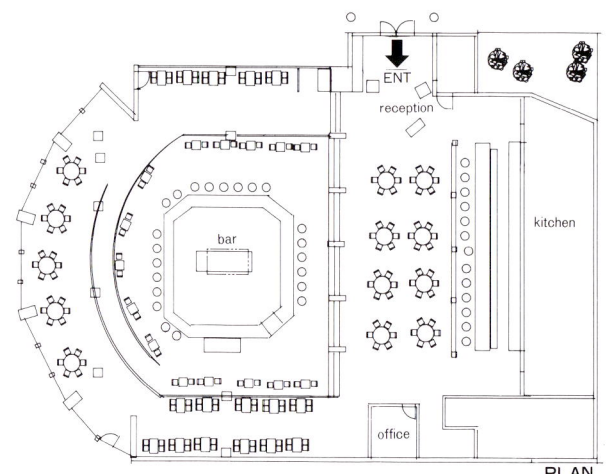

PLAN

⑥

ⓐ

ⓑ

⑦

⑧

ⓒ

4/The entrance hall; "Hot Rod Marlin" welcomes guests.
5/A theme uniform designed in the 1950s style.
6/Changes in the world population, forest area, etc. are indicated on the upper part of the open kitchen.
7/The booth seating corner; the wall is decorated with golden records, a collection of photos of rock singers, etc.
8/The window-side table seating area.

4/エントランスホール マスコットの "Hot Rod Marlin" が歓迎してくれる
5/1950年代がテーマのユニフォーム
6/オープンキッチンの上部には世界の人口の変化や森林の面積などが表示されている
7/ブース席 壁面にはゴールデン レコード ロック歌手の写真コレクションなどが飾られている
8/窓側のテーブル席をみる

●menu
a : The Rock's Grilled Chicken Tostada Salad.
b : Lime Bar-B-Q Chicken.
c : HRC Famous Baby Rock Watermelon Ribs.

CHA CHA CHA Encino
⟨Encino⟩

A Caribbean restaurant situated on a corner of a small shopping center in Encino, San Fernando Valley, where, along with population increases, many restaurants have located. A former fish market has been renovated and turned into this restaurant.
By introducing abundant natural light, the interior is exotically illuminated with colorful chairs, displays featuring a tropical motif, pieces of metal sculpture suspended from the high ceiling, antique maps on the floor, etc. The owner-chef Toribino Prado, who was brought up in a Mexican family by an Italian mother, is creating his own contemporary Caribbean foods.
<CHA CHA CHA Encino>
Address/17499 Ventura Blvd. Encino, CA 91316
Phone/818-789-3600

人口増加とレストランの進出が目立つサンフェルナンド ヴァレィのエンシノの小さなショッピングセンターの一角 フィッシュマーケットだった建物をリニューアルしたカリビアン料理レストラン。
店内には自然光がふんだんに採り入れられ カラフルな椅子 トロピカルをモチーフにしたディスプレイ 高い天井から吊るされたメタルのスカルプチャー 床のアンティーク地図などエキゾチックに演出されている。イタリア人の母を持つメキシコ系の家庭に育ったオーナーでシェフのトリビノ プラド(Toribino Prado)は 独自のコンテンポラリィなカリブ海料理をクリエイティブしている。
〈チャ チャ チャ エンシノ店〉
Address/17499 Ventura Blvd.Encino,CA 91316
Phone/818-789-3600

②

③

④

1/The facade; facing Ventura Blvd.
2/The central part of the dining room; accented with colorful chairs and napkins.
3/The reception and bar areas viewed from the entrance.
4/The bar area.

1/ファサード　Ventura Blvd.に面している
2/ダイニングの中央部　カラフルな椅子やナプキンが配されている
3/エントランスからレセプションとバー方向をみる
4/バーエリアをみる

25

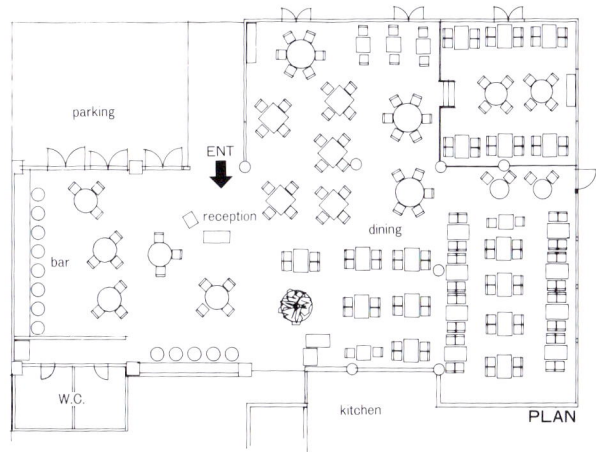

5/ The dining area; an angel sculpture is suspended from the high ceiling.
6/ The ceiling and wall finished with rough-planed lumber; decorated with pieces of art featuring a tropical motif.
7/ The Caribbean antique maps are designed over the entire floor surface.

5/ダイニングをみる 高い天井からエンジェルのスカルプチャーが下がっている
6/荒削りの木を用いた天井と壁面 トロピカルなモチーフのアートが飾られている
7/フロア全体にカリブ海地方のアンティークマップがデザインされている

8/Crew in colorful uniform; the chef-owner Toribio Prado in the center.

● menu
a : Poached Artichoke/Banana Boats/Cucumber Angel Hair Salad.
b : Swordfish Brochette/Salmon En Papaya.
c : Free range Veal Chop/Carioca Chicken.

8/カラフルなユニフォームのクルーたち　中央は　シェフ　オーナーの　Toribio Prado

CHA CHA CHA Long Beach
⟨Long Beach⟩

A restaurant hotly talked about for its Caribbean foods and unique design.
Since the opening of a first restaurant in East Hollywood in 1986, a second restaurant (page 24) opened in Encino in 1991, followed by the opening of this Long Beach restaurant in February 1993.
The design concept common to all three restaurant is the presentation of a Caribbean atmosphere. In this Long Beach restaurant, with blue & green as its basic tones, the interior is uniquely and fantastically presented with lighting of brass coconut trees, paintings in tropical colors and old maps of the Caribbeans drawn on the floor. These were produced by the chef-owner Tribino Prado and his friends.
Situated in downtown Long Beach, this shop which was formerly a gas station, evokes a Latin American church. Provided with a patio, it serves colorful food dishes and various types of drinks in a Caribbean atmosphere.
<CHA CHA CHA Long Beach>
Number of guest seats/140
Address/762 Pacific Avenue Long Beach, CA 90813
Phone/310-436-3900   Fax/310-436-3931

カリブ海地方の料理とユニークな店づくりで話題のレストラン。1986年にイーストハリウッドに1号店をオープン以来 '91年に2号店をエンシノ（本書 24ページ収録） '93年2月にはこのロングビーチ店をオープンさせた。各店共通のデザイン コンセプトはカリビーンの雰囲気の演出であるが ここではブルーとグリーンを基調に ブラスの椰子の木の照明 トロピカルカラーの絵画 床にはカリブ地方の古地図を描くなどユニークでファンタジックにまとめられている。これらはシェフ/オーナーのトリビノ プラド（Tribino Prado）と友人たちによる手づくり。
ロングビーチのダウンタウンに立地するこの店はガソリンスタンドのリニューアルで 中南米の教会のイメージ。パティオが設けられ カラフルな盛り付けの料理やドリンクなど カリブ海の風を感じさせる。
〈チャ チャ チャ ロングビーチ店〉
客席数/140席
Address/762 Pacific Avenue Long Beach, CA 90813
Phone/310-436-3900   Fax/310-436-3931

1・3/The dining area on the patio; with a fountain in the center and leaves of coconut trees painted on the parasol.
2/The facade; styled after a Latin American church.

1・3/パティオのダイニングエリア 中央に泉が設けられ パラソルには椰子の葉が描かれている
2/ファサード 中南米の教会をイメージしている

4/The dining room; gives a fantastic Carribbean atmosphere. Uniquely accented with coconut objet lighting.
5/Shell paintings on the floor and objets on the wall. These objets are also placed on the facade and menu cover as the restaurant's symbol mark.
6/A design on the toilet's wall.

4/ダイニングルーム　カリビーンのファンタジィな雰囲気でまとめている　椰子の照明がユニーク
5/フロアに描かれた貝と壁面のオブジェ
オブジェはシンボルマークとしてファサードやメニューカバーにもデザインされている
6/トイレの壁面のデザイン

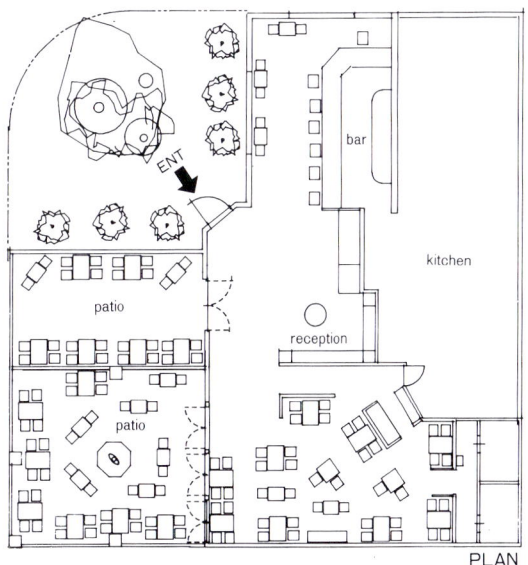

PLAN

7/The bar area viewed from the entrance hall.
8/The colorful reception area of the entrance hall.
9/The bar counter; real leaves of coconut trees are displayed above.
10/Panels of Latin American genre pictures are set in the waist board of the bar counter.

7/エントランスホールよりバーエリアをみる
8/カラフルにディスプレイされた　エントランスホールのレセプションあたり
9/バーカウンター
　上部には本物の椰子の葉が飾られている
10/バーカウンターの腰には中南米の風俗画のパネルがはめ込まれている

● menu
a : ST. BATT'S CURRY SHRIMP.
b : PAELLA CARIBENA.
c : JAMAICAN JEAK CHICKEN/Traditional twice grilled breast of chicken marinated in our secret Jerk spice recipe.
d : CEVICHE GUADALOUPE/Fresh fish marinated in lime juice cilantro and Caribbean spices.

BORDER GRILL
⟨Santa Monica⟩

A Mexican food restaurant opened by the female owner-chefs M. S. Milliken and S. Feniger who also opened "City Cafe" in 1980 in Los Angeles and brought its operation to a success with uniquely cooked contemporary foods. An old warehouse has been renovated into this restaurant. Its design was undertaken by Josh Schweitzer. An "amusing atmosphere" is presented by utilizing the existing space and wall paintings drawn with a unique touch by two artists from London who once designed Sting's album cover.
Thus, "Border Grill" deserves attention as a restaurant whose design concept goes beyond that of the conventional Mexican restaurant design.
<BORDER GRILL>
Number of guest seats/120
Address/1445 4th Street Santa Monica, CA 90401
Phone/213-451-1655

1980年にロサンゼルスに「City Cafe」をオープンし そのコンテンポラリィクッキングのユニークな料理で成功させた女性オーナーシェフ ミリケン（M.S.Milliken）とフェニガー（S.Feniger）のメキシコ料理レストラン。古い倉庫のリニューアルで デザインはジョシュ シュバイツァー（Josh Schweitzer）。既存の空間を生かした店内は 独自のタッチで描かれた壁画で "楽しさ"が演出されている。Sting のアルバムカバーをデザインした 2人のアーティストをロンドンより招き描いたもので 従来のメキシカンレストランのデザインを超えた考え方として注目される。
〈ボーダー グリル〉
客席数/120席
Address/1445 4th Street Santa Monica, CA 90401
Phone/213-451-1655

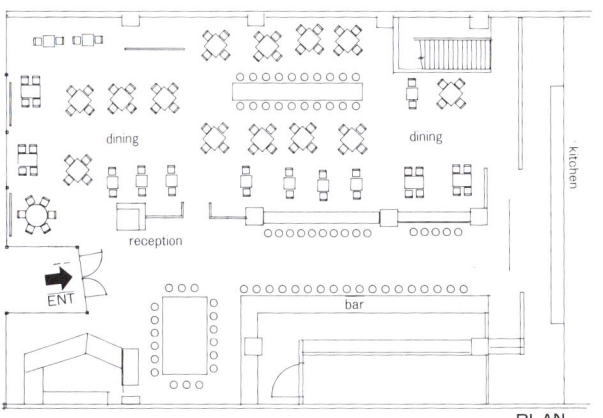

PLAN

1/The bar corner with a large depth; the wall and ceiling are decorated with paintings by Su Huntley and Donna Muir.
2/The dining area.

1/奥行きのある バーコーナーをみる　壁面や天井の絵は Su Huntley と Donna Muir の作品
2/ダイニングエリアをみる

3/The dining room's ceiling paintings.

3/ダイニングの天井画をみる

- menu
- a : Chilled Yucatan Tacos with Shrimp.
- b : Papadzules-Tortilla with roasted Pumpkin seed & Tomato Sauce & Grated Eggs.
- c : Tamales, Guatemalan with Chicken & Olive.

CYPRESS CLUB
⟨San Francisco⟩

Managed by Mr. John M. Cunin, who once managed "Masa's" in San Francisco and has been active in the restaurant business for 20 years, this restaurant adopts a San Francisco style and introduces a bar into the dining area, while arranging the 1940s motif into a contemporary style.
Lighting that evokes parachutes, cylindrical marble pillars, a balloon-like copper arch, mohair chairs, mosaic floors, etc. All these elements contribute to giving the interior a fantastic atmosphere. Designed by Jordan Mozer, who asserts that the design "should have a personality like that of a friend." Young chef Cory Schreiber's cuisine features simple and refined tastes which may be said to be "American brasserie food" centering around seafoods.
<CYPRESS CLUB>
Number of guest seats/186 (restaurant 144, bar 42)
Address/500 Jackson Street San Francisco, CA 94133
Phone/415-296-8555

サンフランシスコの「Masa's」の元マネジャーでレストランビジネス20年のジョン カニン（Jhon M. Cunin）が経営するこのレストランは バーをダイニングの中にとり入れたサンフランシスコスタイルで 1940年代のモチーフを現代風にアレンジしたデザインが特徴。パラシュートをイメージさせる照明 円筒形のマーブルの柱 気球のような銅製のアーチ モヘアのチェアー モザイクのフロアなどファンタスティックなインテリアでまとめている。デザインは"レストランは友人と同じようにパーソナリティを持つべきだ"と主張する ジョーダン モザー（Jordan Mozer）。料理は若きシェフ コリィ シュレイバー（Cory Schreiber）で シーフードを強調したアメリカン ブラッセリィとでもいう シンプルで洗練された味を提供している。
〈サイプレス クラブ〉
客席数/186席（レストラン 144席　バー 42席）
Address/500 Jackson Street San Francisco, CA 94133
Phone/415-296-8555

1/The bar on the left side of the entrance; with a bar tool in the shape of a wine cask.
2/The club room; mainly used for dinner parties.
3/The central part of the dining room; the balloon-shaped copper arch leads to the club room.
4/The facade.

1/エントランス左手のバー　ワイン樽をイメージしたバーツールが置かれている
2/クラブルーム　主に会食に利用される
3/ダイニングルームの中心部　中央の気球をイメージしたコパー（銅）のアーチはクラブルームへの入口
4/ファサード

③

to kitchen
raised floor dining
closet
bar
main floor dining
club room
(private party)
raised floor dining
ENT
PLAN

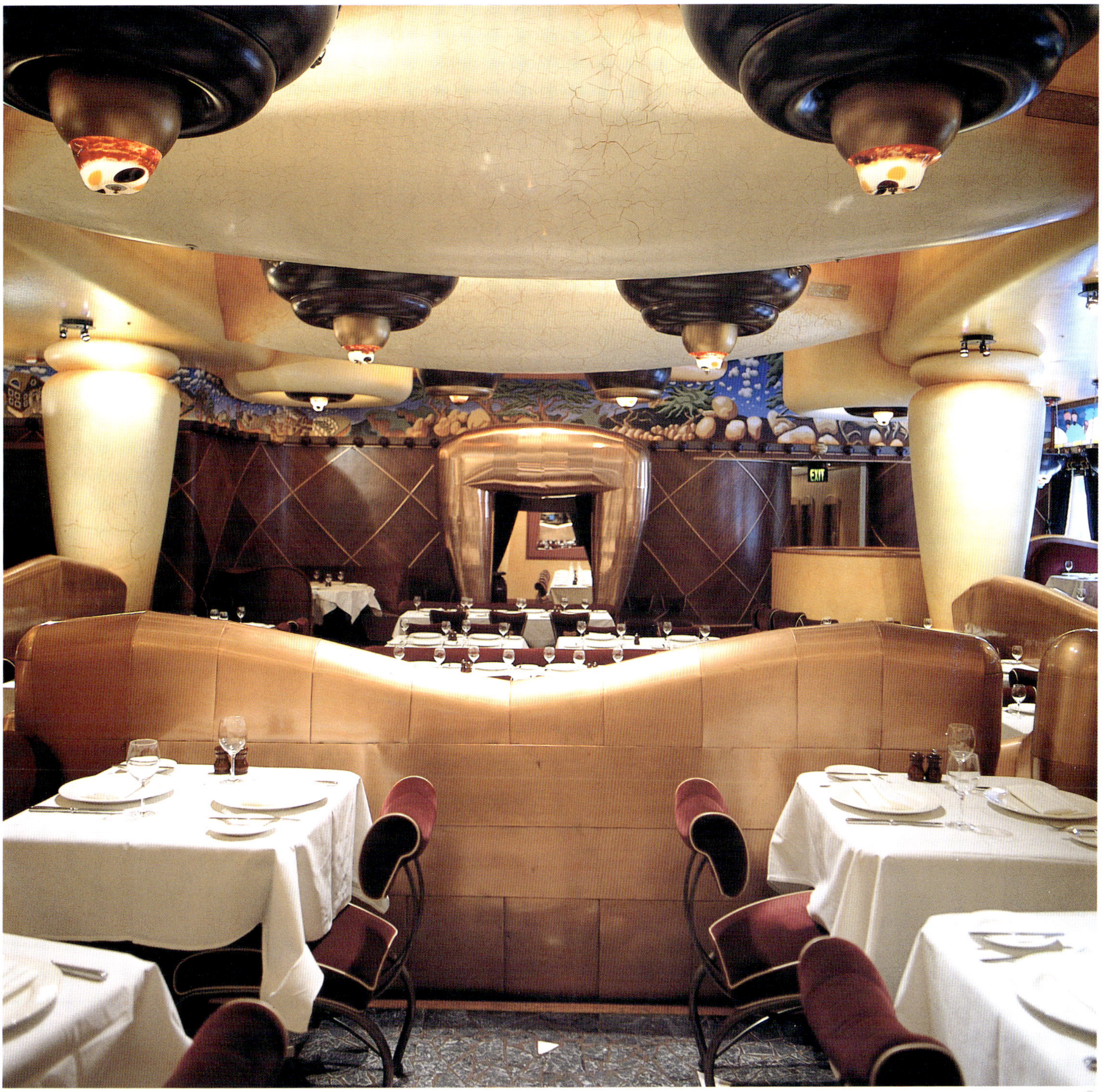

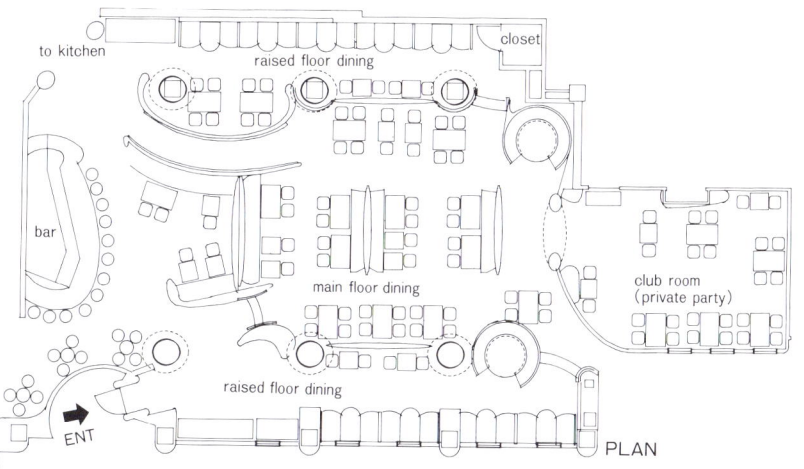

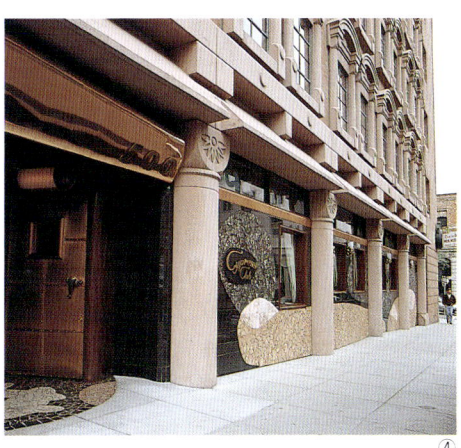

④

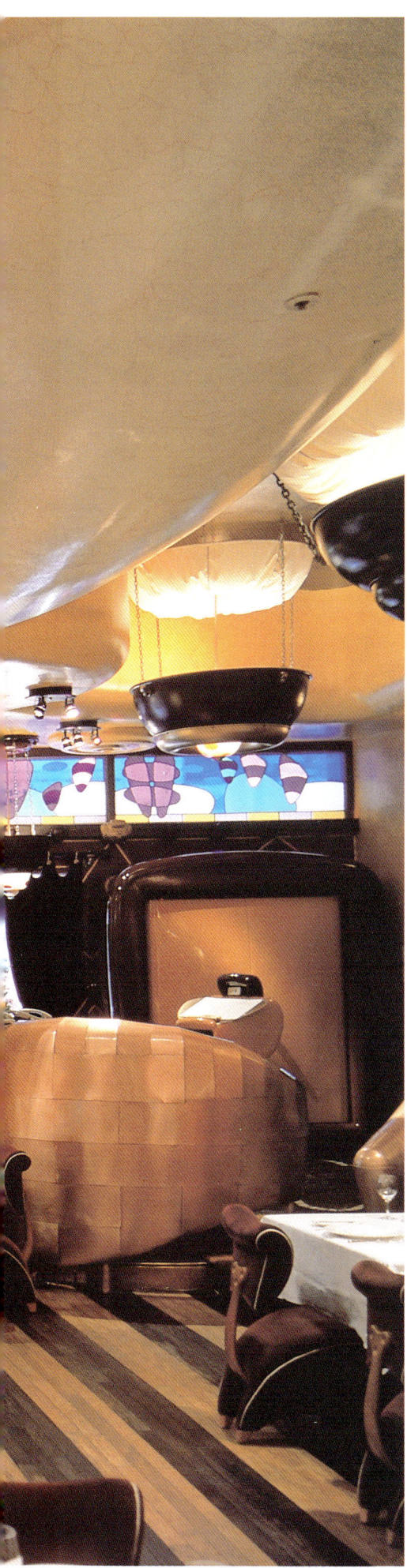

5/The central part of the dining room; the reception desk is visible on the right side. Designed with lighting, pillars, etc. in 1940s style.

● menu
a : Crispy salmon and potato cake with citrus marinated vegetables.
b : Roasted snapper with grapefruit, tarragon and a crispy noodle cake.
c : Chocolate Toffee Torte.

5/ダイニングの中心部　右側にレセプションをみる
照明や柱など1940年台のデザインでまとめている

CAFE LA BOHEME
⟨West Hollywood⟩

The first shop opened overseas by Hasegawa Jitsugyo (headquartered in Tokyo) which is developing "Cafe La Boheme" (mainly serving pasta foods) and "Zest" (serving Tex-Mex foods) chains in Tokyo. The shop design was undertaken by Margaret O'Brien. According to her, she attempted to "express a fantasy consisting of time and place which have not existed in the past nor will exist in the future, and thereby create an ultimate stage for eating as an image dedicated to great Hollywood." Objets were made by Ren Makabe. The chef is Koichiro Kikuchi who is serving creative and novel dishes called "California Eclectic."

⟨CAFE LA BOHEME⟩
Number of guest seats/180 (dining 145, patio 35)
Address/8440 Santa Monica Blvd. West Hollywood, CA 90069
Phone/213-848-2360   Fax/213-848-9447

現在 東京・首都圏でパスタ料理を中心とした「カフェ ラ ボエム」とテックスメックス料理の「ゼスト(Zest)」をチェーン展開する 長谷川実業(本社・東京)の海外出店の1号店。デザインはマーガレット オブライエンで 中世ヨーロッパの城をイメージの基本に"過去にも未来にも存在しない時間と場所からなる幻想を表現 偉大なるハリウッドに捧げたオマージュとしての究極の食の舞台である"と語る。オブジェは真壁 廉。シェフは菊地晃一郎で"カリフォルニア エクレクティック"と呼ぶクリエイティブで斬新な料理を提供している。

⟨カフェ ラ ボエム⟩
客席数/180席(ダイニング 145席　パティオ 35席)
Address/8440 Santa Monica Blvd. West Hollywood, CA 90069
Phone/213-848-2360   Fax/213-848-9447

1/The reception and bar viewed from the entrance area.
2/The entrance area accented with moon and star objets.
3/The high-ceiled dining area; with an image of bodhisattva produced by Ren Makabe.

1/エントランスあたりからレセプションとバーをみる
2/月と星のオブジェがあるエントランス廻り
3/高い天井のダイニングをみる　菩薩像は真壁 廉の作品

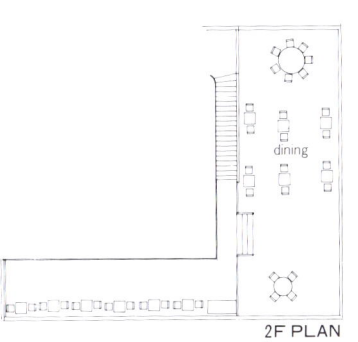
2F PLAN

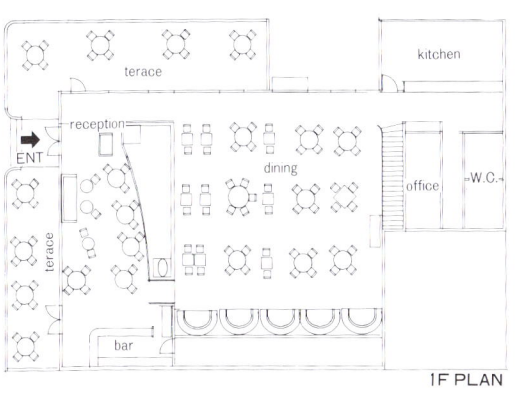
1F PLAN

●menu
a : Smoked Tuna with Julienne Vegetables Wasabi Sauce and Mint Puree.
b : Stuffed Free Range Chicken, Steamed Rice and Sweet Potato Meilfeuille, Jalapeno and Tomato Sauce.
c : Grilled Salmon and Steamed Mussels and Squid, Two kind baure blanc with Torteilla Salad.
d : Challatte Chocolate with Creme Anglaise.

4/メザニン席よりダイニングを見おろす
5/1階　カーテンで仕切られたブース席とカーテンのだまし絵のある2階席をみる
6/バーとダイニングエリアの中間に設けられたモザイクタイル貼りの池

4/The dining area overlooked from the mezzanine seating area.
5/The 1st floor; a booth seating area partitioned by a curtain and the 2nd floor seating area with a trompe l'œil of curtain.
6/A mosaic tiled pond installed between the bar and dining areas.

SCHATZI ON MAIN
<Santa Monica>

Being managed by Arnold Schwarzenegger, this restaurant was designed by Adam D. Tihany. It is composed of a terrace, open kitchen and dining room equipped with a bar. The interior, which features a bricked ceiling and large columns, is designed with casual lighting, booth seating area, etc.
Here, eclectic foods based on French dishes are served. Due to the reasonable and affordable prices, "Schatzi On Main" is popular as a community-friendly restaurant.
<SCHATZI ON MAIN>
Number of guest seats/120 (dining 90, patio 30)
Address/3110 Main Street Santa Monica, CA 90405
Phone/310-399-4800

アーノルド シュワルツェネッガー（Arnold Schwarznegger）経営のレストランで 設計はアダム ティハニー（Adam D.Tihany）。テラス オープンキッチン バーを備えたダイニングルームで構成されており ブリックの天井と大きな円柱がある店内は照明 ブース席などカジュアルなデザインでまとめられている。
料理はフランス料理をベースにしたエクレクティックなもので リーズナブルでアフォーダブルな価格設定で地域密着型のレストランとして人気を得ている。
〈シャッツィ オン メイン〉
客席数/120席（ダイニング 90席　パティオ 30席）
Address/3110 Main Street Santa Monica, CA 90405
Phone/310-399-4800

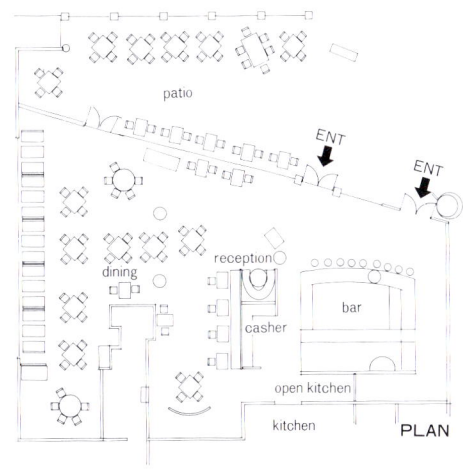

1/The reception and dining areas viewed from the bar area.
2/Guest seats on the garden patio viewed from the entrance.
3/The service area behind the dining area.

1/バーエリアからレセプションとダイニングをみる
2/エントランスからガーデンパティオの客席をみる
3/ダイニング奥のサービスエリア

④

4/The bright dining area giving an image of the Mediterranean Sea.
5/A table seating area facing the garden patio; the partition is accented with colored glass.
6/Uniform expressing casualness and youthfullness.

4/地中海をイメージさせる明るいダイニング
5/ガーデンパティオに面したテーブル席をみる　パーティションに色ガラスでアクセントをつけている
6/カジュアルさと若さを表現したユニフォーム

⑤

⑥

●menu
a : Crab Blintz with Tomato Salsa & Cole Slaw.
b : Halibut Crusted with White & Black Sesame Seeds served over Rice with Sunomono, Baby Bok Choy and Yellow Squash, with Ginger Soy Sauce.
c : Maria's Oriental Chicken Salad with Sesame Dressing.
d : Apple Strudel with Vanilla Ice Cream.

BAYSIDE 240
⟨Redondo Beach⟩

A seafood restaurant situated on Redondo Beach, a resort about 10 km south of Los Angeles International Airport facing the Pacific Ocean. Managed by "Portofino Inn Hotel."
Here, 12 types of fresh seafood are served everyday. These foods are cooked by incorporating unique features of Italian, American, Chinese and Mexican dishes. The interior has a casual resort atmosphere, designed originally with an open kitchen which is nearly 10 m long, a bar accented with a sea serpent objet made by using driftwood, and a dining area with a 5 × 30 feet fresco whose theme is the sea and waves.
<BAYSIDE 240>
Number of guest seats/200 (restaurant 125, bar 75)
Address/240 Portofino Way Retondo Beach, CA 90277-2092
Phone/213-374-8043

ロサンゼルス国際空港の南約10kmの太平洋に面したリゾート地　レドンドビーチにあるシーフードレストラン。経営は「ポートフィノ インホテル(Portofino Inn Hotel)」。
料理は　毎日12種類のフレッシュな魚介類を取り揃えたシーフードで　イタリアン　アメリカン　チャイニーズ　メキシカンの料理の特徴を取り入れたユニークなコンセプト。店内はリゾート感覚のカジュアルなインテリアで　10m近くもあるオープンキッチン　流木で造った海蛇のオブジェがあるバー　海と波をテーマにした　5×30フィートの壁画のあるダイニングエリアなど　独創的なデザインのレストランである。
〈ベイサイド 240〉
客席数/200席(レストラン 125席　バー 75席)
Address/240 Portofino Way Retondo Beach, CA 90277-2092
Phone/213-374-8043

1/The dining room; the painting on the wall picturing the sea and waves is by Joe Monroe.
2/The bar area; the sea serpent objet above the counter, which is made of driftwood, has become a mascot.
3/The facade; facing the Pacific Ocean.

1/ダイニングルーム　壁面の海と波をイメージした絵はジョー モンロー(Joe Monroe)の作品
2/バーエリア　カウンター上部の流木を利用した海蛇のオブジェ　マスコットになっている
3/ファサード　太平洋に面している

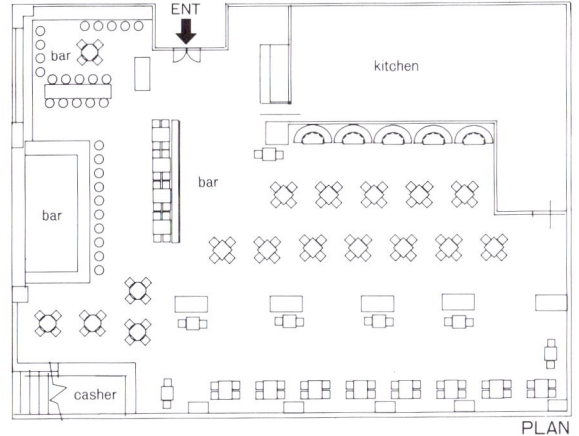

4/The terrace seating area and dining room from which guests can command a 180° view of outside scenery.
5/Tables on the booth seating area; wave patterns are designed by using maple.
6/The reception desk, behind which the open kitchen can be seen.

4/テラス席とダイニングルーム　180度の展望が楽しめる
5/ブース席のテーブル　カエデ製で波のパターンがデザインされている
6/レセプションテーブル　奥はオープンキッチン

● menu
a : GRILLED LOBSTER PASTA.
b : NORTHWEST KING SALMON/Grilled with Artichoke Puree and white wine.
c : SMOKED SALMON PIZZA.

RED CAR GRILL
⟨West Hollywood⟩

Modeled after a passenger car on the California Railways which have been widely known as the "Red Car," this restaurant mainly offers oven and grilled foods cooked in an open kitchen. Designed by Pat Kuleto, a designer who is active mainly in San Francisco, the interior reproduces the gorgeous atmosphere of the good old "Red Car" by using mahogany, brass, parquet, etc.
⟨RED CAR GRILL⟩
Number of guest seats/154 (restaurant 142, bar 12)
Address/8571 Santa Monica Blvd. West Hollywood, CA 90069
Phone/213-652-9263

"レッド カー"の愛称で親しまれたカリフォルニア鉄道の客車を模したインテリアのこのレストランは オープンキッチンで調理されるオーブンとグリル料理がメイン。サンフランシスコを中心に活躍する建築家 パット クレート（Pat Kuleto）の設計で マホガニー ブラス 寄せ木などの素材で 古き良き "レッド カー"をしのばせるゴージャス感を再現している。
⟨レッド カー グリル⟩
客席数/154席（レストラン 142席 バー 12席）
Address/8571 Santa Monica Blvd.West Hollywood,CA 90069
Phone/213-652-9263

1/The open kitchen and main dining area; imaging an early station of California Railways.
2/The dining area imaging a dining car of "Red Car."
3/The facade.
4/The open kitchen and counter seating area; an upper range hood looks like a steam locomotive.

1/オープンキッチンとメインダイニングをみる　カリフォルニア鉄道の初期のころの駅をイメージしている
2/レッドカーの食堂車をイメージしたダイニング
3/ファサード
4/オープンキッチンとカウンター席　上部のレンジフードは蒸気機関車のようでもある

⑤

⑥

⑦

⑧

● menu
a : Grilled Skewers, Seasonal Vegetables.
b : Chopped Vegetables & Wild Rice Salad.

5/The bar area.
6/The counter top; finished with marble.
7/The booth seating area.
8/The service station.
9/The open kitchen; serving grills in the main.

5/バーエリアをみる
6/カウンタートップ　大理石を用いている
7/ブース席をみる
8/サービスステーション
9/オープンキッチン　グリル料理がメイン

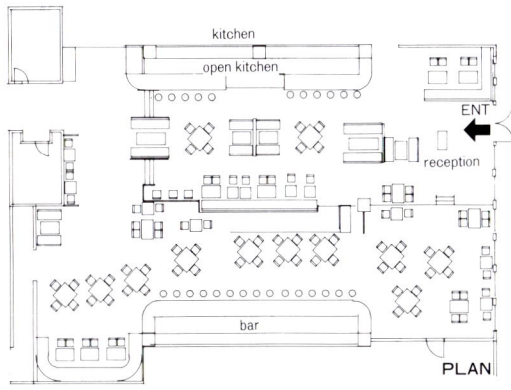

BLACKHAWK GRILL
⟨Danville⟩

This restaurant is situated in Danville which is known as a high class residential quarter about 30 minutes by car from downtown San Francisco. Danville is continuing to grow due to reasons such as the opening of a building complex composed of a shopping center, offices, specialty shops, automobile museum, etc.
The "Blackhawk Grill" is managed by the California Cafe Restaurant Corporation which is developing 14 shops mainly in California. Its menu features ethnic foods, such as grills, pastas, pizzas and salads, cooked in an open kitchen by utilizing local fresh materials. Mainly by combining pastel, wood and earth tones, the interior is presented as a bright space by introducing light from large windows and a skylight. Also, by tying up with the Behring Auto Museum which is also in the same complex building, classic cars are displayed in the interior space, thus gaining popularity.
⟨BLACKHAWK GRILL⟩
Number of guest seats/230 (dining 150, patio 50, bar 30)
Address/3540 Blackhawk Plaza Circle, Danville, CA 94506
Phone/415-736-4295

サンフランシスコのダウンタウンから車で約30分　高級住宅地として知られるダンヴィルに立地する。ショッピングセンター　オフィス　専門店　自動車博物館などで構成するコンプレックスビルのオープンなどでますます発展を続けている地区である。経営はカリフォルニアを中心に14店を展開するカリフォルニア　カフェ　レストランコーポレーション。オープンキッチンの開放感と　新鮮な地場の食材を活かしたグリル　パスタ　ピザ　サラダなどマルチエスニックなメニュー構成が特徴。
インテリアはパステル　ウッド　アーストーンなどを組み合わせ　大きな窓にスカイライトを取り入れた明るい空間にまとめている。また同コンプレックス内にある　Behring Auto Museum と提携　店内にクラシックカーを展示　好評を得ている。
⟨ブラックホーク　グリル⟩
客席数/230席（ダイニング　150席　パティオ　50席　バー　30席）
Address/3540 Blackhawk Plaza Circle, Danville, CA 94506
Phone/415-736-4295

1/ The entrance hall and bar counter viewed from the bar lounge.
2/ The bar area near the entrance; accented with a display of classic car.
3/ The facade and patio; situated within a shopping center.

1/バーラウンジからエントランスホールとバーカウンターをみる
2/エントランス近くのバーエリア　クラシックカーが展示されている
3/ファサードとパティオ　ショッピングセンター内に立地する

④

4·5/The high ceiling and dining area with unique walls; provided with an open kitchen.
6/The service area on the guest seating space; harmoniously combined with the open kitchen.

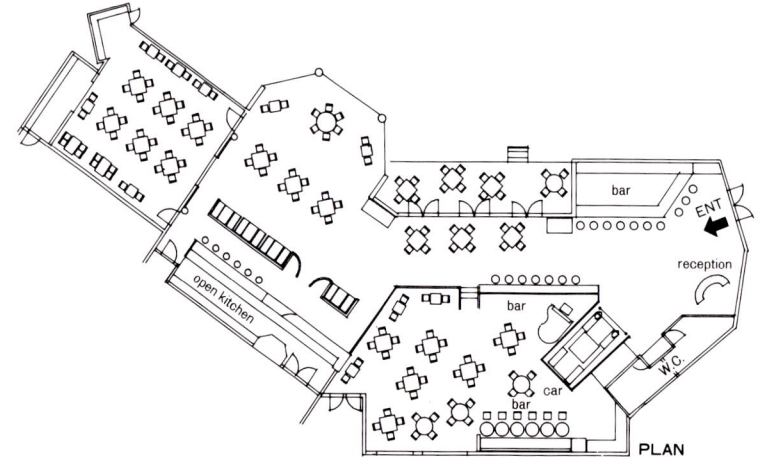

4·5/高い天井と特徴のある壁面のダイニング　オープンキッチンが設けられている
6/客席　サービスエリア　オープンキッチンがうまく組み合わされている

● menu
a : Corn fried Fresh Soft Shell Crab, Cabbage Salad & Sundried Tomato, Aioli.
b : Steamed White Asparagus, warm Pink Pepper Corn, Confit of Duck & Orange Vinaigrette.
c : Pan seared Salmon, Fried Celery Root Basil Oil, Red & Yellow Cherry Tomatoes.

RESTAURANT LULU
⟨San Francisco⟩

The areas around the Convention Center in San Francisco is called "South of Market," where offices, restaurants, etc. have advanced one after another in recent years. A warehouse having 83 years of history has been renovated into "LuLu" which features a bright space. It was designed by Sam Lopata which is a representative American designer mainly active in New York.

The interior space is designed by imaging the Piazza Campidoglio by Michelangelo, and features a semi-circular ceiling using thick fir boards. An open kitchen, installed behind the central part of the interior space, is equipped with a large wood-fired rotisserie for firewood and a painted duct. The bar counter's top uses leather and the design is composed of Italian touch elements. The menu items are centered around popular French and Italian foods which can be enjoyed casually in a seaside atmosphere.

Managed by Louise "LuLu" Clement and the chef Reed Hearon.

<RESTAURANT LULU>
Number of guest seats/165 (dining 140, bar 25)
Address/816 Folsom St. San Francisco, CA
Phone/415-495-5775

サンフランシスコのコンベンション センター周辺は "サウス オブ マーケット" と呼ばれ 近来 オフィスやレストランの進出が目立つ地域でこの「ルル」も83年の歴史を持つ倉庫をリニューアルしたもので 明るい空間を持つレストランである。設計はサム ロパタ(Sam Lopata)で 彼はニューヨークを中心に活躍するアメリカの代表的なデザイナー。
店内はミケランジェロのカンピドグリオ広場(Piazza Campidoglio)をイメージした店づくりで 樅の木の厚板を用いた半円形の天井が設けられている。中央部奥はオープンキッチンで 大きな薪用のロティスリー(wood-fired rotisserie)やペイントされた排煙ダクトがある。バーカウンターのトップにはレザーが使用されるなど イタリアンタッチのデザインで構成されている。料理はフランスやイタリアのシーサイド感覚の手軽に楽しめるものが中心になっている。
経営はルイス ルル クレメント(Louise "LuLu" Clement)とシェフのリード ハーロン(Reed Hearon)。

⟨レストラン ルル⟩
客席数/165席(ダイニング 140席 バー 25席)
Address/816 Folsom St.San Francisco,CA
Phone/415-495-5775

①
②

1/The reception area viewed from the entrance.
2/The dining area whose floor is lower than the surrounding space.
3/The bright dining area into which natural light is introduced; the entrance area viewed from an inner part.
4/The facade; the entrance is equipped with a slope.
5/The dining area and bar.

1/エントランスからレセプション方向をみる
2/フロア ダウンしたダイニングエリア
3/自然光を採りいれ明るいダイニング 店内奥からエントランス方向をみる
4/ファサード エントランスにスロープが設けられている
5/ダイニングとバーをみる

● menu
a : Grilled Asparagus with Lemon & Olive Oil.
b : Iron Skillet Roasted Mussels, La Cagouille Style.
c : Frito Misto of Artichokes with Fennel and Parsley.
d : Warm Shellfish Salad with Lemon & Olive Oil.
e : Grilled Jumbo Rib Steak Florentine Style with Tuscan Beans (Serves Two).
f : Rosemary Scented Roast Chicken with Warm Tomato and Winter Lettuce Salad.

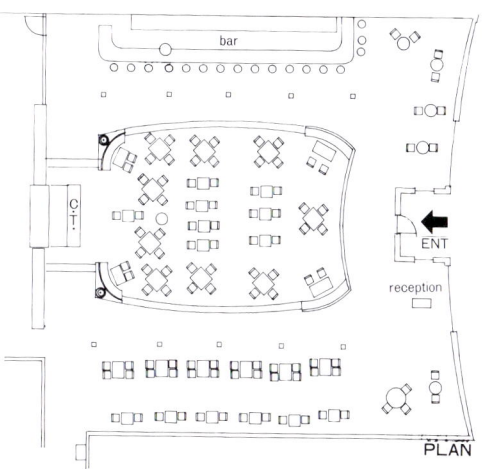

PLAN

6/The open type dining area which was a warehouse before renovation; provided with a rotisserie for firewood in the center.
7/The joint managers, Louise "Luku" Clement (left) and the chef Reed Hearon.

6/倉庫をリニューアルした開放的なダイニング 中央に薪用のロティスリーがある
7/共同経営者の Louise "LuLu" Clement(左) と シェフの Reed Hearon

65

TERRAZZA TOSCANA
⟨Encino⟩

An Encino shop of "Trattoria Toscana" which is the most popular Italian restaurant in Los Angeles, "Terrazza Toscana" is situated on the 2nd floor of a shopping center.
The interior is designed in an informal, countrylike atmosphere and very bright. Designed by Sam Lopata. Equipped with an open kitchen having a large pizza oven and a bar corner, "Terrazza Toscana" is constructed in an orthodox style. It has a patio seating area provided with heating equipment, and also a takeout corner whose concept is the same as "Rosti," a sister takeout shop.
An increasing number of famous restaurants from Los Angeles have advanced into the Encino area, offering their dishes at reasonable prices. In this restaurant, too, traditional Tuscan foods are gaining popularity lunch as served at $15 and dinner at $26 to $27.
<TERRAZZA TOSCANA>
Number of guest seats/206 (dining 138, patio 48, bar 20)
Address/17401 Ventura Blvd. Encino, CA 91316
Phone/818-905-1641

ロサンゼルスで最も人気のあるイタリア料理レストラン「トラットリア トスカーナ(Trattoria Toscana)」のエンシノ店でショッピングセンターの2階に立地している。
店内はインフォーマルなカントリー調の雰囲気を持ち明るい。デザインはサム ロパタ(Sam Lopata)。大きなピザオーブンを備えたオープンキッチンやバーコーナーもあり 本格的な造りのレストランになっている。ヒーティング設備のあるパティオ席も用意され 姉妹店のテイクアウトショップ「ロスティ(Rosti)」と同じコンセプトのテイクアウトコーナーも併設している。
このエンシノ地区にはロサンゼルスからの有名店の進出が目立ち リーズナブルな価格で料理を提供しているが この店でもランチ 15ドル ディナー26～27ドルの伝統的なトスカーナ地方の料理が人気をあつめている。
〈テラッツァ トスカーナ〉
客席数/206席(ダイニング 138席　パティオ 48席　バー 20席)
Address/17401 Ventura Blvd. Encino, CA 91316
Phone/818-905-1641

1/The dining area and an order counter with a wine cabinet; the floor is finished with terracotta tiles.
2/The open kitchen; with a wood burning pizza oven in the center.

1/ダイニングとワインキャビネットのあるオーダーカウンターをみる 床はテラコッタ タイル
2/オープンキッチンをみる 中央にウッドバーニングピザオーブンが設けられている

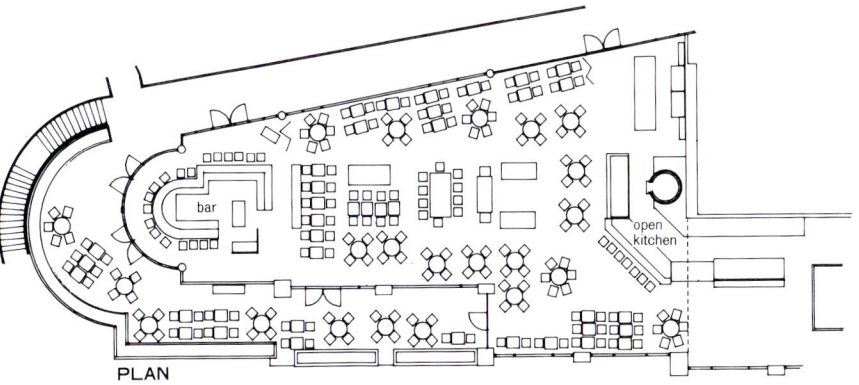

PLAN

ⓒ

ⓐ

ⓑ

3/An antipasto buffet installed in the center of the dining room and crew; the ceiling lighting is custom-made.
4/The facade; situated on the 2nd floor of Courtyard Shops SC.
5/The patio's dining area.
6/The service station.
7/The horseshoe-shaped bar counter near the entrance.

3/ダイニングルームの中央に設けられたアンティパストのブッフェとクルーたち　天井の照明はカスタムメイド
4/ファサード　コートヤード　ショップスＳＣの2階にある
5/パティオのダイニングエリア
6/サービスステーションをみる
7/エントランス近くの馬蹄形のバーカウンター

⑦

●menu
a : INSALATE MARE/mixed seafood salad.
b : FIORENTINA/large T-bone steak cooked in our wood burning oven.
c : RISOTTO ALLA CATALANA/risotto with shrimp & saffron.

McCORMICK & KULETO'S SEAFOOD RESTAURANT
⟨San Francisco⟩

A seafood restaurant having 450 guest seats — one of the largest seating capacities in San Francisco. Situated on Chirardelli Square, a tourist spot, it is favorably accepted by local guests and tourists. The building was formerly used by "Maxwell's Plum" which was known as an ultra gorgeous art deco restaurant, and after its withdrawal, it has been renovated into this seafood restaurant.
It is successfully developing a community-friendly operation by offering a moderately priced seafood menu (comprising about 110 items) — unit price per customer is $15 for lunch and $29 for dinner.
Jointly managed by McCormick & Schmick Managing Group which is operating 11 seafood restaurants and 2 nightclubs across the U.S.A., and Mr. Pat Kuleto, an architect who has undertaken the shop design.
<McCORMICK & KULETO'S SEAFOOD RESTAURANT>
Number of guest seats/450
Address/900 North Point Street San Francisco, CA 94109
Phone/415-929-1730

サンフランシスコで最大級の450席を誇るシーフードレストラン。観光名所であるギラデリー スクエア(Ghirardelli Square)に立地し 地元客やツーリストに好評である。
この場所はかつて アールデコの超豪華レストランで知られた「Maxwell's Plum」だった所で 撤退後にリニューアルしたもの。
モデレート プライスのシーフードメニュー(約110アイテム)を提供し客単価をランチ15ドル ディナー29ドルにおさえた地元密着型の展開で成功している。
全米で 11のシーフードレストランと 2つのナイトクラブを運営するMccormick & Schmick マネージング グループと設計を担当した建築家のパット クレート(Pat Kuleto)氏の共同経営。
〈マッコーミック&クレートズ シーフードレストラン〉
客席数/450席
Address/900 North Point Street San Francisco, CA 94109
Phone/415-929-1730

①

②

③

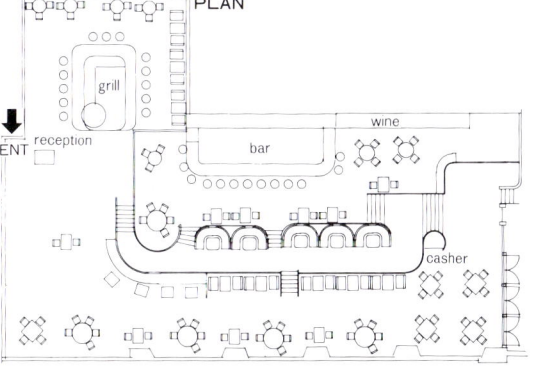

PLAN

1/ The Crab Cake Lounge near the entrance; with an oven installed in the cafe style interior space.
2/ The entrance to the Crab Cake Lounge which looks like a sunroom.
3/ The appearance of Ghirardelli Square; the restaurant is situated on the 2nd floor of this building.
4/ The dining area; the interior gives an image of the 1920s. Lighting is impressive.

1/エントランス近くの Crab Cake Lounge　カフェスタイルの店内にオーブンを設けている
2/サンルーム風のCrab Cake Lounge への入り口
3/ギャラデリー スクエアの外観　この建物の2階がレストラン
4/ダイニングをみる　1920年代をイメージさせるインテリアで照明が印象的

5/The bar lounge viewed from the dining area.
6/The bar corner; teak is used on the floor.

5/ダイニングからバーラウンジをみる
6/バーコーナーをみる　床にはチーク材が使用されている

●menu
a : Ahi and Mahi Mahi with Mango Chutney Barbeque Glaze.
b : Smoked Lobster, Pear and Radiccio Salad.
c : Pacific Seafood Stew.

ETRUSCA
⟨San Francisco⟩

An Italian restaurant taking up the culture and art of the Etruscan people who are said to have lived in the middle western part of Italy in 900 B.C.
In the interior space, wall and ceiling paintings representing Etruscan culture are painted, showing a sharp contrast with the modern appearance of the building. The interior featuring a heavy use of maple and mahogany gives a composed atmosphere, coupled with onyx lighting appliances suspended from the ceiling. In an open kitchen which can be looked into through a glass partition, innovative North Italian foods are cooked by using a three-layered roasting oven.
<ETRUSCA>
Number of guest seats/115
Address/121 Spear Street San Francisco, CA 94105
Phone/415-777-0330

紀元前900年に イタリアの中西部に住んでいたというエトルリア人の文化や芸術をテーマにしたイタリア料理レストラン。
店内には エトルリア文化を表した壁画や天井画がデザインされ近代的なビルの外観とは対象的である。楓やマホガニィを多用したインテリアや天井から吊り下げられたオニキスの照明機器が落ち着いた雰囲気を醸し出している。ガラスのパーティション越しに眺められるオープンキッチンにある3層のロースティングオーブンを使用した 革新的な北イタリア料理を提供している。
〈エトラスカ〉
客席数/115席
Address/121 Spear Street San Francisco, CA 94105
Phone/415-777-0330

1/ Looking up at the bar area from the dining area; the bar area is higher by 4 feet than the dining area.
2/ The dining area; designed by imaging the Etruscan culture in ancient Italy.
3/ The restaurant's facade accented with a tent; situated on the 1st floor of the redeveloped Rincon Center 11.
4/ The bar's entrance viewed from the reception area; on the left side there are wall paintings expressing the Etruscan culture.

1/ダイニングからバー方向を見上げる　ダイニングエリアより4フィート高い
2/ダイニング　古代イタリアのエトルリア文化をイメージしデザインされた
3/テントのあるレストランのファサード　再開発されたRincon Center 11のビルの1階にある
4/レセプションあたりからバーの入口をみる　左側にはエトルリア文化を表現した壁画がある

⑤

5/The marble-topped U-shaped bar counter behind which lies the dining area.

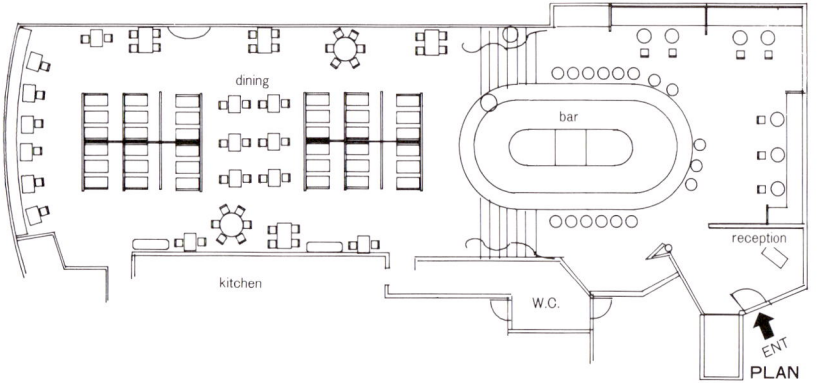

5/マーブルトップのU字形のバーカウンター 奥はダイニングエリア

●menu
a : Mozzarella Alla Romana.
b : Coniglio Al Forno Con Funghi.
c : Storione Con Spugnole.
d : Fili di Marroni.

I CUGINI TRATTORIA
⟨Santa Monica⟩

An Italian restaurant opened on the 1st floor of a new office building in Santa Monica and managed by the University Restaurant Group.
Having 250 seats, the wide interior space is designed by reproducing ancient Italy with a cafe-like atmosphere. The dining area, finished with abundant marble and cherry, is composed of a market corner for takeouts, open kitchen, bar, etc. The menu combines traditional Italian local foods and Californian foods with a light taste. Cooked by the chef Rebecca Matarazzi.
⟨I CUGINI TRATTORIA⟩
Number of guest seats/250 (incl. patio)
Address/1501 Ocean Avenue Santa Monica, CA 90401

サンタモニカの新しいオフィスビルの1階にオープンしたイタリア料理レストラン。経営はユニバーシティ レストラン グループ社。
パティオ席を含む250席の広い店内は イタリアの古い時代をイメージしたデザインで カフェの雰囲気。ダイニングには大理石や桜材を多用しテイクアウトのマーケットコーナー オープンキッチンとバーなどで構成されている。料理は伝統的なイタリアの地方料理とライト感覚のカリフォルニア料理を組み合わせたメニューでシェフは Rebecca Matarazzi。
⟨イ クジーニ トラットリア⟩
客席数/250席(パティオ席を含む)
Address/1501 Ocean Avenue Santa Monica, CA 90401

①

②

1/The facade; situated on the 1st floor of an office building facing the Ocean Avenue.
2/The patio seating area; covered with large sheets of glass.
3/The market corner near the entrance.
4/The central part of the dining area; guests can enjoy viewing the patio and sea through the glass.
5/An inside view of the open kitchen.
6/The open kitchen viewed from the service station.

③

1/ファサード オーシャン アベニューに面したオフィスビルの1階にある
2/パティオ席 大きなガラスで覆われている
3/エントランス近くのマーケットコーナー
4/ダイニングエリアの中央部をみる ガラス越しにパティオと海が眺められる
5/オープンキッチンの内側をみる
6/サービスステーションからオープンキッチンをみる

④

⑤

⑥

⑦

7/The dining room; imaging the ancient Italy.
8/The reception area and bar corner.

7/ダイニングルーム　イタリアの古い時代をイメージしている
8/レセプションとバーコーナーをみる

● menu
a : Antipasto della Casa, Assorted meats and prepared vegetables.
b : Nodino, Large veal chop grilled with fresh herbs & lemon.

(a)

(b)

81

IL FORNAIO CUCINA EXPRESSA
⟨Costa Mesa⟩

A quick service restaurant opened on a corner in Costa Mesa, South California, which is crowded with shopping centers, art centers, business complexes, etc. Managed by Il Fornaio (headquartered in San Francisco) which is also operating Italian bakeries and restaurants. Through semi-self service eat-in and takeout delivery, "Il Fornaio Cucina Expressa" can quickly serve high-quality foods from the morning, noon and nighttime menus.
As one enters the restaurant, one sees a service line consisting of menu-wise corners for drinks, dishes, desserts, etc. When a guest receives drinks, foods, etc. from the respective corners and pays for them at the cashier desk, a host or busboy guides the guest to his seat while carrying his tray.
⟨IL FORNAIO CUCINA EXPRESSA⟩
Address/650 Anton Blvd. Costa Mesa, CA
Phone/714-668-0880　Fax/714-668-0440

南カリフォルニア　コスタメサのショッピングセンター　アートセンター　ビジネスコンプレックスなどが集まる一画にオープンしたクイックサービスのレストラン。イタリアンベーカリーとレストランのイル フォナイオ（本社・サンフランシスコ）の経営。セミセルフサービスのイートインとテイクアウト　デリバリーといった方法で　朝　昼　夜ごとのメニューをクイックサービスでハイクォリティの料理を提供している。
エントランスを入ると　サービスラインに飲み物　料理　デザートなどメニューごとのコーナーが設けられており　各コーナーで商品を受け取り　キャッシャーで支払いを済ますと　ホストやバスボーイが席までトレイを持って案内してくれるというシステム。
イタリアの市場感覚を取り入れた店づくりでまとめている。
⟨イル フォナイオ クチーナ エキスプレッサ⟩
Address/650 Anton Blvd. Costa Mesa, CA
Phone/714-668-0880　Fax/714-668-0440

1/The terrace seating area covered with a white tent.
2/The high-ceiled dining room.
3/A signboard beside the entrance.
4/The facade.

1/白いテントで覆われたテラス席
2/高い天井のダイニングルーム
3/エントランス脇のサインボード
4/ファサード

DOLCI
PASTA
PIETANZE
EXIT

⑤

CT
ENT
patio
open kitchen
office
PLAN

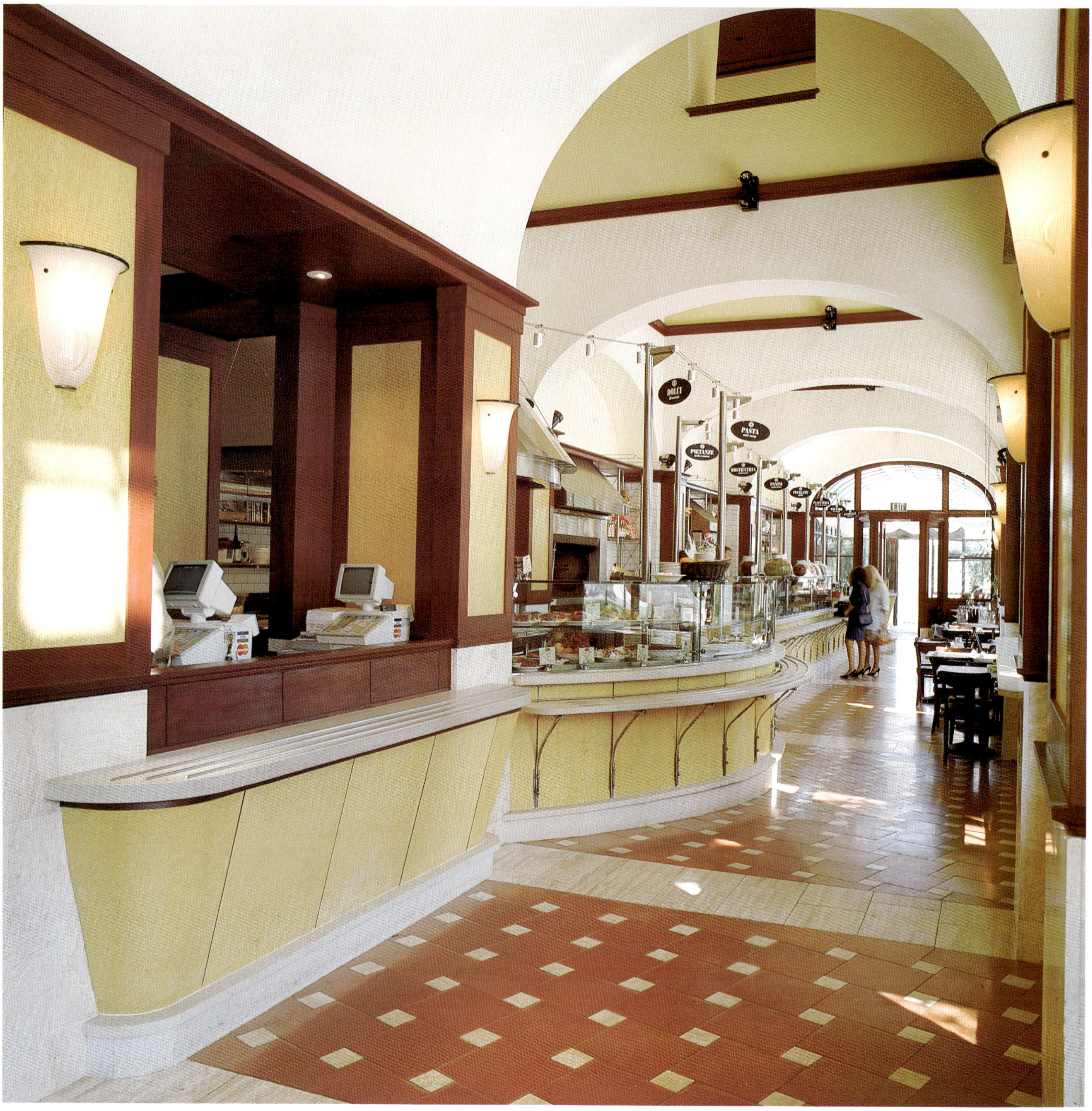

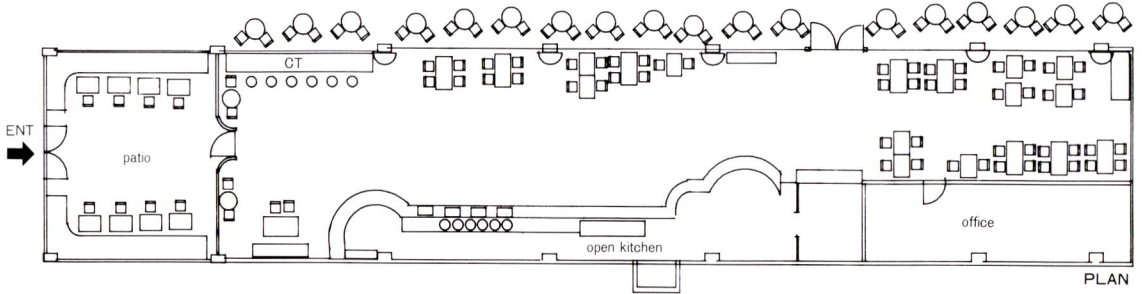

5/The counter service lane running from the entrance viewed from the cashier desk.
6/Salad and sandwich corners viewed from the service area.
7/The counter upon which trays are placed in a row; from this section, the counter leads to drinks, bread, salad, main dish and dessert corners.

5/キャッシャーからエントランス方向 カウンターサービスのレーンをみる
6/サラダ類とサンドイッチ類のコーナーをサービスエリアからみる
7/トレイが並ぶカウンターをみる ここからドリンクスやパン サラダ メイン料理 デザートコーナーへと続く

BROADWAY DELI
⟨Santa Monica⟩

A deli restaurant opened on a corner of a redeveloped promenade on the 3rd St. in Santa Monica. New York is the home of delis which were originally patronized by Jews. This restaurant offers a menu introducing various types of tastes from different parts of the world (21 types of main courses and 18 types of sandwiches). The interior space (about 330 m²) is composed of selling corners, bar and dining area. A selling corner near the entrance, which occupies about 1/3 of the total space, features a display of eating materials ordered from various parts of the world. The square bar counter is installed in the center, while the restaurant with its casual atmosphere is secured behind the bar counter, and a long counter seating area runs beside the open kitchen.
<BROADWAY DELI>
Address/1457 3rd St. Promenade Santa Monica, CA 90401

サンタモニカの3番街(3rd St.)の再開発されたプロムナードの一画にオープンしたデリレストラン。デリカはニューヨークが本場で ユダヤ人の食べ物であったが この店では世界のいろいろな味を取り入れたメニュー(メインコース21種 サンドイッチ18種類)を提供している。
約330㎡の店内は 販売コーナー バー ダイニングエリアで構成され 全体の1/3のスペースを占める エントランス付近の販売コーナーでは世界各地から集めた食材を並べている。中央部は四角いバーカウンター その奥がレストランでカジュアルな雰囲気でまとめられ オープンキッチンの脇は 長いカウンター席になっている。
〈ブロードウェイ デリ〉
Address/1457 3rd St.Promenade Santa Monica,CA 90401
Phone/213-451-0616

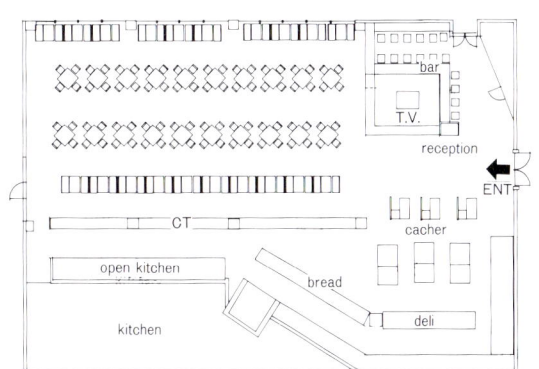

1/The deli selling corner.
2/The bar corner in the center; equipped with TV monitors, it has a casual atmosphere.
3/The facade.

1/デリの販売コーナー
2/中央のバーコーナー　ＴＶモニターがありカジュアルな雰囲気
3/ファサード

4/The bright dining area with glass tables.
5/The fresh deli corner.
6/The homemade bread corner.
7/Looking across the counter into an inner part of the dining area.

4/ガラスのテーブルがある明るいダイニングエリア
5/フレッシュなデリのコーナー
6/ホームメイドのパンコーナー
7/カウンター越しにダイニング奥をみる

⑦

a

b

● *menu*
a : Smoked Norwegian Salmon with Bagel Bread.
b : Hot Pastrami Sandwich.

CALIFORNIA BEACH ROCK N' SUSHI
⟨Los Angeles⟩

A bright and colorful sushi shop with a beach motif, it is situated along fashionable Melrose Ave in Los Angeles. In the restaurant, rock is on the air as BGM, and the interior space is mainly composed of a wide, spectacular dining area, counter, bar corner and terrace near the entrance which represents a beach.
The counter is equipped with a water tube in which water bubbles up attuning to rock. Coupled with the coloring, this sushi shop features a brand-new design and a menu that is quite different from that of conventional sushi shops, thus becoming the talk of the town.
<CALIFORNIA BEACH ROCK N' SUSHI>
Address/7656 Melrose Los Angeles, CA

ビーチをテーマにした明るくカラフルなスシ店で ファッショナブルなロサンゼルスのメルロース通り（Melrose Ave.）沿いに立地している。
ＢＧＭにロックが流れる店内は 広くスペクタクルなダイニングエリア カウンター バーコーナー エントランス付近のビーチを表現したテラスなどで構成されている。カウンターにはロックに合わせて水が泡立つウォーターチューブが設けられ カラーリングも含め従来のスシ店のイメージとは全く異質のデザインとユニークなメニュー構成で話題を呼んでいる。
〈カリフォルニア ビーチ ロックン スシ〉
Address/7656 Melrose Los Angeles, CA
Phone/213-655-0123

①

②

③

④

⑤

1/ The facade.
2/ The entrance hall area imaging waves on the sea.
3/ The interior space is colorful; provided with TV monitors, the interior gives an image quite different from that of conventional sushi shops.
4/ The center with a water tube on the wall of the counter seating area; water bubbles up in attunement with rock.
5/ The interior space whose theme is the sea and rock; wall paintings by Doug Kanegawa stand out.

1/ファサード
2/海の波をイメージしたエントランスホールあたり
3/店内はカラフル ＴＶモニターが設けられ従来のスシ店のイメージを変えている
4/中央 カウンター席の壁面にはウォーターチューブが設けられロックに合わせ水が泡立つ演出をしている
5/海とロックがテーマの店内 Doug Kanegawa の壁画が目立つ

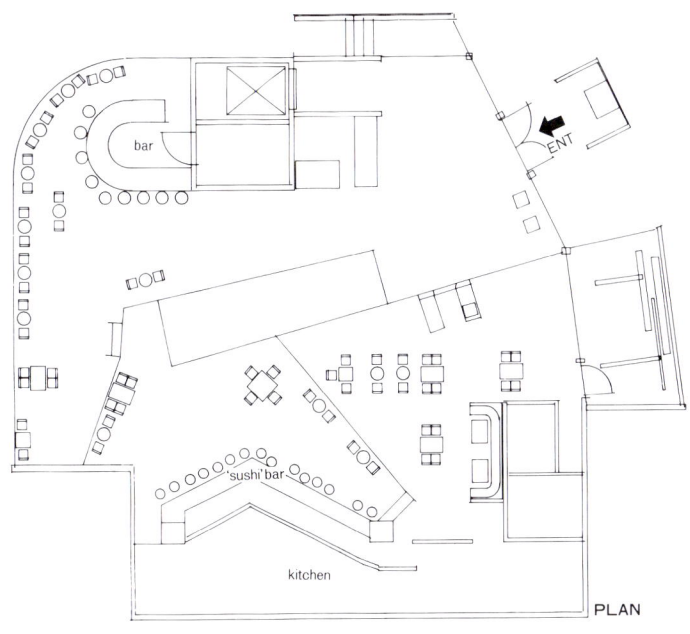

PLAN

⑥

6/The counter seating area and entrance area.
7/Movement and conversations of crew also stir up the shop's atmosphere.
8/The bar corner.
9/The bar corner viewed from the window side.

6/カウンター席とエントランス方向をみる
7/クルーたちの動きや会話もこの店の雰囲気を盛り上げる
8/バーコーナー
9/窓側からバーコーナーをみる

⑦

92

⑧

⑨

ⓐ

ⓑ

ⓒ

● menu
a : Philadelphia Roll.
b : Caterpillar Roll.
c : Sunshine Roll.

THE STINKING ROSE
⟨San Francisco⟩

As the unique name suggests, "THE STINKING ROSE" is a restaurant specializing in garlic dishes. The owner, Jerry Dal Bozzo has spent about 10 years studying all available data on garlic, thus bringing America's only garlic food restaurant into being.
On the facade, garlic farms in Gilroy, a district famous for garlic production, are painted, and 150 garlic products are sold.
The central bar corner is decorated with an exquisite model of a garlic factory and the ceiling features a display of bulbs. In the banquet room on the 2nd floor, paintings, with garlic as a theme, were done on the wall by a local painter.
The menu is composed of items which incorporate a new sense of North Italian foods and utilize the Californian ingredients.
⟨THE STINKING ROSE⟩
Number of guest seats/205 (dining 125, banquet room 80)
Address/325 Columbus Ave, San Francisco, CA 94133
Phone/415-781-7673

"悪臭を発する薔薇"というユニークな店名の ガーリック料理専門のレストラン。オーナーの Jerry Dal Bozzo は 約10年間をかけ ガーリックについてのすべての資料を研究したというアメリカ唯一のこだわりレストランである。
外観には産地として有名なギロイ(Gilroy)のガーリック畑が描かれ 店内のコーナーでは150アイテムのガーリック商品が販売されている。
中央のバーコーナーには精巧なガーリック工場の模型が飾られ 天井には球根がディスプレイされている。2階のバンケットルームには 地元の画家によるガーリックをテーマにした壁画か描かれているなど インテリアから料理まですべて ガーリックをテーマにしている。料理は特に北イタリア地方料理の新しい感覚を取り入れ カリフォルニアの食材を活かしたメニュー構成をしている。
⟨ザ スティンキング ローズ⟩
客席数/205席(ダイニング 125席 バンケットルーム 80席)
Address/325 Columbus Ave, San Francisco, CA 94133
Phone/415-781-7673

①

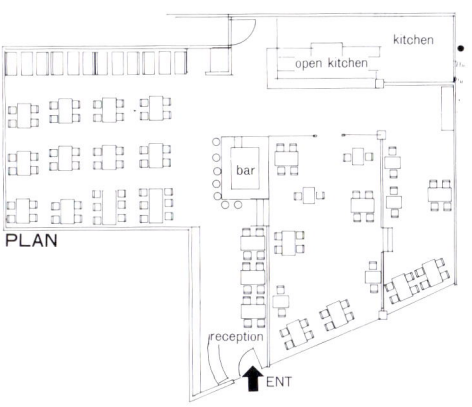

1/The bar counter; the model of a garlic factory in Rube Goldberg style displayed above.
2/The 1st floor; The dining room.
3/The facade.

1/バーカウンター 上部にRube Goldbergスタイルのガーリック工場の模型が飾られている
2/1階 ダイニングルーム
3/ファサード

4/The 2nd floor; the banquet room with Chuck Kennedy's interesting illustration.
5/The wall of the staircase area.
6/(from right to left) Joint managers Dante Serafini and Dean Dal Bozzo, and chef Robert Larman.

4/2階 バンケットルーム　Chuck Kennedy のイラストが面白い
5/階段廻りの壁面をみる
6/右から 共同経営者の Dante Serafini, Dean Dal Bozzo とシェフ Robert Larman

●menu
a : Giant Salt roasted Prawns with Garlic Herb Butter served with Garlic Herb Pasta.
b : Whole Dungeness Crab oven roasted in Garlic and Extra Virgin Olive oil.
c : Garlic Sausage Pizza.
d : Black Lobster Ravioli with Safron Cream and fried White Garlic Chive.

CAFE VALLARTA
⟨Santa Barbara⟩

This restaurant takes the name of a Mexican port as its own, since the owner, Justo G. Gracia, came from Vallarta which is the sister city of Santa Barbara.
Since it is situated in this quiet town whose population is only about 90,000 and which is blessed with a rich natural landscape bordered by the sea and surrounded by mountain, and is only 7 blocks away from the downtown area, the restaurant is also endeavoring to increase demand for catering and party services.
Joint manager Liliana Parra is well known for having won the championship at various cooking contests, and playing a central role when undertaking everything from cooking to planning.
From the facade to the interior, a white and blue tone is used and Mexican folk-aft articles are displayed, thus creating a homely atmosphere.
The menu is composed of traditional Mexican and Yucatan foods which are cooked without using any lard or artificial seasonings.
<CAFE VALLARTA>
Number of guest seats/105 (dining 75, patio 30)
Address/626 E. Haley Street Santa Barbara, CA 93103
Phone/805-564-8494

メキシコの港町を店名にしたレストラン。サンタバーバラの姉妹都市でありオーナーのユスト グラシア(Justo G.Gracia)の出身地であることに由来する。
海や山の自然に恵まれた人口9万人ほどの静かなこの町の ダウンタウンまで 7ブロックという立地もあり この店ではケイタリングやパーティの需要にも力をいれている。
共同経営者のリリアナ パルラ(Liliana Parra)は種々の料理コンテストに優勝し有名だが 調理から企画まですべて彼女が中心になってサービスしている。ファサードから店内まで白とブルーを基調にまとめ メキシコの民芸品などが飾られ 家庭的な雰囲気を醸し出している。
メニューは伝統的なメキシコ料理とユカタン地方の料理で構成し ラードや人工調味料は一切使用していない。
⟨カフェ バヤルタ⟩
客席数/105席(ダイニング 75席　パティオ 30席)
Address/626 E.Haley Street Santa Barbara,CA 93103
Phone/805-564-8494

1/The dining room.
2/The bar viewed from the inner dining room.
3/The restaurant's entrance area.
4/The inner dining room's entrance area.

1/ダイニングルームをみる
2/奥のダイニングからバーをみる
3/レストランへの入り口廻り
4/奥のダイニングへの入り口廻り

Puerto Vallarta.
Sebastian
SABATER

⑤

CAFÉ VALLARTA
OPEN

⑥

patio
ENT
office
bar
kitchen
PLAN

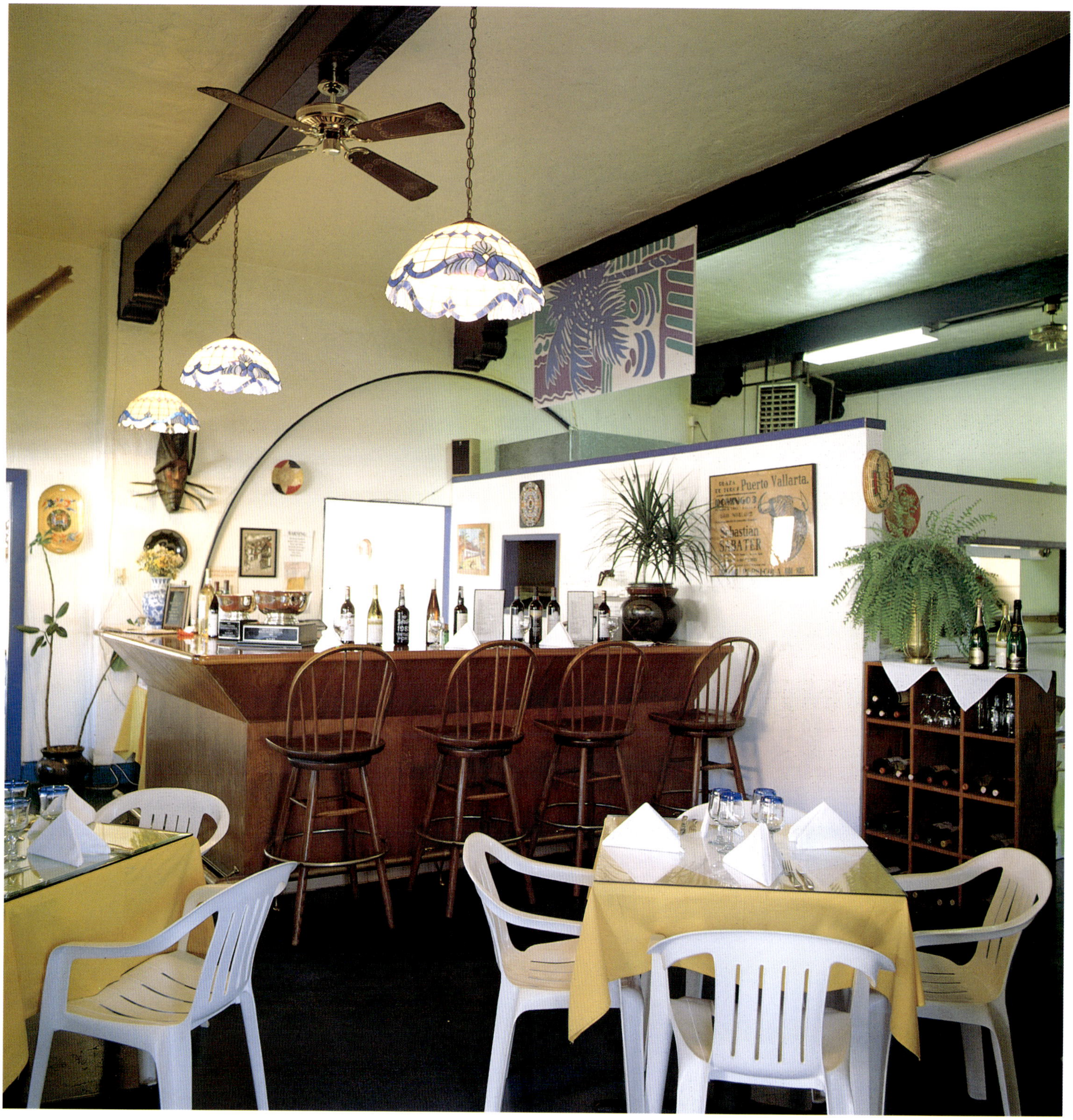

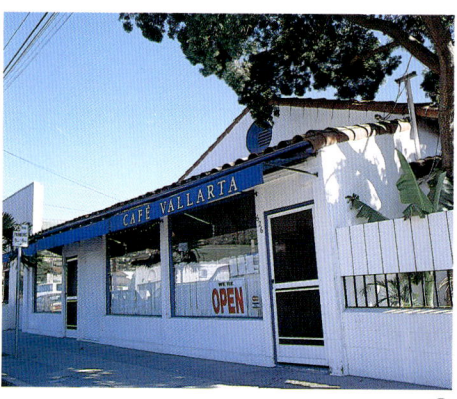

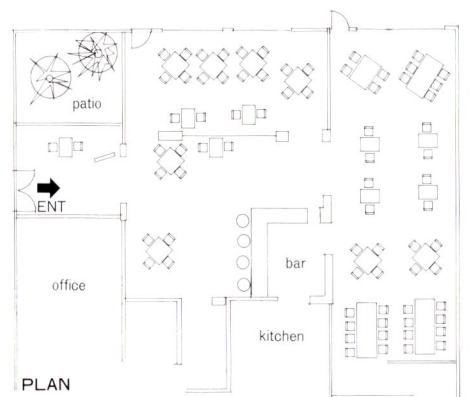

5/The bar viewed from the dining room.
6/The facade.
7/The owner Justo G. Gracia (left) and Liliana Parra.

5/ダイニングからバーをみる
6/ファサード
7/オーナーの Justo G.Gracia(左)と Liliana Parra

● menu
a : Culiacan Style Prawns, Stuffed with Herbs & Cheese & Wrapped in Bacon.
b : Chile Relleno Calamari.
c : Chocolate Flan with Cream Anglaise & Chocolate Shavings.

FAMA
⟨Santa Monica⟩

An Italian restaurant which opened in downtown Santa Monica, South California, where redevelopment is underway.
It was designed by David Kellen who succeeded in making a unique shop by using maple veneer. By utilizing the characteristics of this finishing material, he used irregular shapes to create a particularly relaxed space which cannot be produced by straight lines, while cutting down on the interior cost.
Managed by Mr. and Mrs. Röckenwagner, "FAMA" offers a menu composed of 4 types of salads, 7 types of appetizers, 8 types of home-made pastas, 2 types of day-by-day pizzas, and 3 types of main courses. These are priced from $5 to $14 and are served in a homely and friendly atmosphere.
<FAMA>
Number of guest seats/117 (dining: 1st floor 75, 2nd floor 32, bar: 10)
Address/1416 4th Street Santa Monica, CA 90401
Phone/213-458-6704

再開発が進む南カリフォルニアのサンタモニカのダウンタウンにオープンしたイタリア料理レストラン。
デザインは David Kellen で楓のベニヤ材を用いたユニークな店づくりをしている。素材のもつ特性を活かし イレギュラーな形を表現することで 直線にない特別な親しみを感じさせる空間にまとめ上げると同時に内装費の削減も図っている。
経営はレッケンバグナー(Röckenwagner)夫妻で 料理はサラダ類4種 アペタイザー7種 ホームメイドのパスタ8種 日替りピザ2種 メインコース3種の構成で 5〜14ドルの価格帯で提供。家族的でフレンドリーなサービスを感じさせる。
〈ファーマ〉
客席数/117席（ダイニング 1階 75席 2階 32席 バー 10席）
Address/1416 4th Street Santa Monica, CA 90401
Phone/213-458-6704

①

1/The reception area; the wall color images the sea.
2/Overlooking the dining room whose interior is designed with irregular veneer materials.
3/The facade.
4/The bright dining room facing the street.

1/レセプション廻りをみる　壁面の色は海をイメージしている
2/イレギュラーなベニヤ材でデザイン構成されたダイニングを俯瞰する
3/ファサード
4/通りに面した明るいダイニング

5/The bar corner uniquely accented with maple veneer pillars and beams.

5/楓のベニヤ材の柱や梁がユニークなバーコーナー

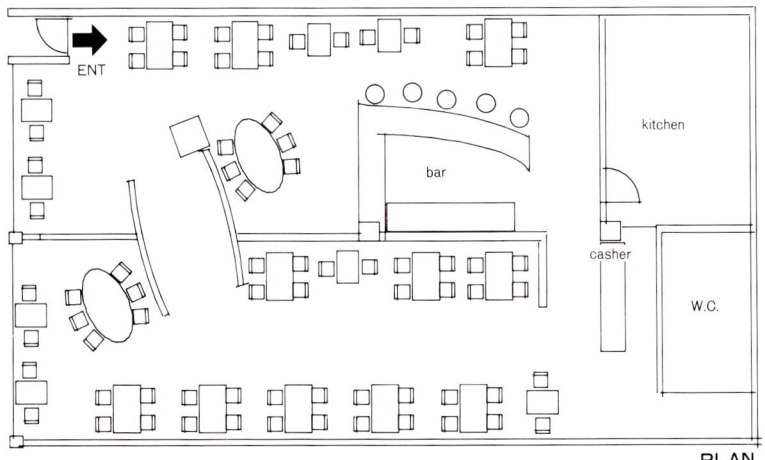

PLAN

●menu
a : Roasted Peppers and Pine Nuts on a Green Salad.
b : Ricotta-Filled Ravioli with Fresh Tomato Sauce.
c : Fresh sauteed Louisiana Gulf Shrimp on Basil Fettuccine with Home-cured Tomatoes and Lobster, Butter Sauce.
d : Capri Salad-Tomato Sauce, Fresh Basil, Fresh Mozzarella Tomato Concasse.

REMI
⟨Santa Monica⟩

The shop name "REMI" means a gondola oar and real oars are used as ceiling decoration. It was designed by Adam D. Tihany who wished to produce the image of a European coastal resort restaurant. In contrast to the terrace seating area which looks like a casual cafe into which the bright Californian sun shines, the interior space features a high ceiling under which the dining room extends in an atmosphere that is quite relaxed due to the lighting and colors which bring back memories of Venice.
The restaurant serves North Italian foods cooked by the chef Antonucci who was born in Venice. They are characterized by the heavy use of fish.
<REMI>
Address/1451 3rd Street Promenade Santa Monica, CA 90401
Phone/213-393-6545

店名の「レミ」はゴンドラのオールのことで 天井の装飾用に本物が使用されている。デザインはアダム ティハニー(Adam D.Tihany)でヨーロッパの海岸のリゾート レストランをイメージした演出をしている。テラス席はカリフォルニアの太陽の下で明るい光がさしこむカジュアルなカフェといった感じであるが 店内は天井が高くヴェニスの光と色を感じさせる落ちついた雰囲気のダイニングルームが広がっている。料理はヴェニス生まれのシェフ アントヌッチ(Antonucci)の伝統的な北イタリア料理で 魚介類が多いのが特徴。
⟨レミ⟩
Address/1451 3rd Street Promnade Santa Monica,CA 90401
Phone/213-393-6545

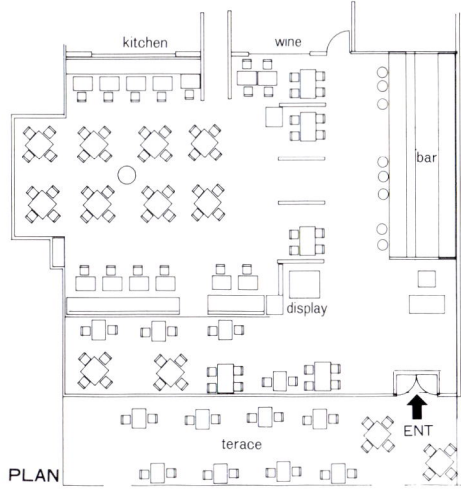

1/ The facade with a terrace seating area which looks like a cafe.
2/ The bright dining room decorated with "remis" on the ceiling.
3/ The dining room partitioned by a long seating area with chairs to secure an area like a sunroom.

1/カフェのようなテラス席のあるファサード
2/天井に"レミ"を飾った明るいダイニング
3/ダイニングの長い椅子席をパーティションにし サンルームのようなエリアを設けている

④

⑤

⑥

⑦

4/The interior space features light which reminds us of Venice.
5/A wine cellar visible across the wall glass.
6/The bar viewed from a private room which also serves as a wine cellar.
7/Crew wearing a striped shirt and uniform tie.

4/店内はヴェニスの光を感じさせる
5/壁面のガラス越しにワインセラーがみえる
6/ワインセラーを兼ねたプライベートルームからバーをみる
7/ストライプのシャツと揃いのネクタイ姿のクルーたち

109

MISS PEARL'S JAM HOUSE
⟨San Francisco⟩

This restaurant, which is said to have a Caribbean theme, features a tropical design presenting an island resort atmosphere with colorful pieces of custom furniture, a glass-top bamboo bar, and bright Jamaican genre pictures. Reggae is on the air as BGM.
It specifically serves spicy island cuisine in the tropical Californian style.
It is managed by Chip Conley who also operates the adjacent hotel "The Phoenix Inn." The chef is Joey Altman. In the morning, the restaurant is frequented by hotel guests.
⟨MISS PEARL'S JAM HOUSE⟩
Number of guest seats/140 (dining 90, bar 50)
Address/601 Eddy Street San Francisco, CA 94109
Phone/415-775-5267

カリブ海をイメージしたというこのレストランは カラフルなカスタム ファニチュア グラストップのバンブーバー 明るいジャマイカの風俗画など アイランド リゾートの雰囲気を演出したトロピカルなデザインでまとめられている。ＢＧＭにはレゲエが流されている。
料理はトロピカルなカリフォルニア風で スパイスのきいたアイランド クイジーンが特徴。
経営は隣接するホテル「The Phoenix Inn」と同じ チップ コンレイ(Chip Conley)。シェフはジョーイ アルトマン(Joey Altman)。
朝はホテルの宿泊客用に使用される。
⟨ミス パールス ジャム ハウス⟩
客席数/140席(ダイニング 90席 バー 50席)
Address/601 Eddy Street San Francisco, CA 94109
Phone/415-775-5267

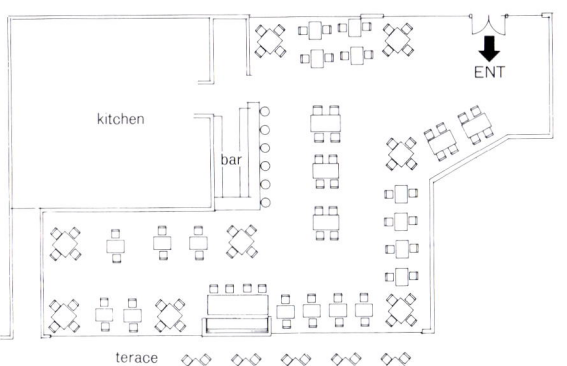

1·2/The dining room featuring a tropical presentation, and walls.

PLAN

1·2/トロピカルに演出されたダイニングと壁面をみる

3·4/The dining room designed by using images of the Caribbean Sea and corner seating area which reminds us of an island resort scene.
5·6/Crew in T-shirt uniform and the chef Joey Altman known for his creative foods.

3·4/カリブ海地方のイメージが演出されたダイニングルームとアイランド リゾートの風景を思わせるコーナー席
5·6/Tシャツのユニフォーム姿のクルーたちと　クリエイティブな料理で話題のシェフ　Joey Altman

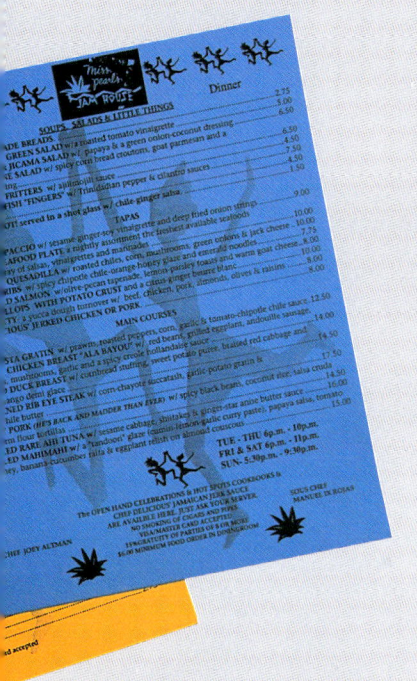

● menu
a : Shrimp + Crab Etoufee with Artichokes/Peas, Crab filled Eggplant cup.
b : Island Pepperd Beef Salad with grilled Chayote-Corn Salsa + Buttermilk fried Okura.
c : Seared Scallops with Potato Crust and a Citrus-ginger Beurre Blanc.

DALE'S BISTRO
⟨Los Angeles⟩

This is a bistro type restaurant standing in the face of La Cienega Blvd. in Los Angeles which is crowded with unique galleries, etc.
The bright white walled interior space is divided lengthwise into two areas — i.e. the entrance side and its opposing (left) side — and decorated with posters and paintings. Thus, it looks like a gallery. The motto of the owner-chef Dale Payne is to offer quality foods and services at reasonable prices.
The restaurant serves unique cuisine by blending traditional French foods with the essence of Californian and other Pacific Rim foods. They are moderately priced from $3.50 to $13 so that guests can order several dishes and nibble at each one.
＜DALE'S BISTRO＞
Number of guest seats/50
Address/361 N. La Cienega Blvd. Los Angeles, CA
Phone/213-659-3996

ユニークなギャラリーなどが集まるロサンゼルスのラ シエネガ通り（La Cienega Blvd.）に面して建つビストロタイプのレストラン。
白壁の明るい店内は エントランス側とその左側の縦に二分された構成で ポスターや絵画が飾られギャラリー風なインテリアでまとめられている。オーナーでシェフのデイル ペイン（Dale Payne）のモットーは 安い価格で質の高い料理とサービスを提供することで 伝統的なフランス料理にカリフォルニアなど環太平洋（パシフィックリム）のエッセンスをブレンドした独自の料理を売り物にしている。価格を3.50～13ドルの巾におさえ 数種類の料理をオーダーするグレージング感覚を大切にしている。
〈デイルズ ビストロ〉
客席数/50席
Address/361 N.La Cienega Blvd.Los Angeles,CA
Phone/213-659-3996

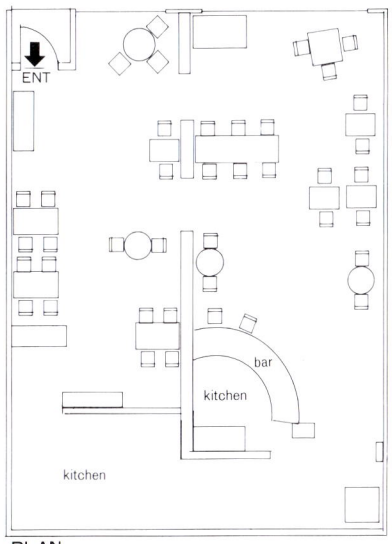

1/ The facade featuring a showy iron artwork.
2/ The dining room on the entrance side which gives an image of a restaurant within an art gallery.
3/ An iron signboard above the entrance.

1/鉄製のアートワークが目立つファサード
2/アートギャラリーの中のレストランをイメージさせる
　エントランス側のダイニングルーム
3/エントランス上部の鉄製のサインボード

PLAN

④

⑤

⑥

⑦

ⓐ

ⓑ   ⓒ

● menu
a : CHINESE CHICKEN SALAD.
b : TUSCAN CHICKEN SANDWICH WITH ROASTED PEPPERS.
c : WON-TONS STUFFED WITH ESCARGOT.

4/The dining room on the left side of the entrance; in a "post-modern bistro" style.
5-7/Marty Cure's pieces of work decorated on the wall.
8/The owner-chef Dale Payne.

4/エントランス左側のダイニング　ポスト　モダンの
　　ビストロ風の造り
5-7/壁面に飾られた Marty Cure の作品
8/オーナー　シェフ　Dale Payne

117

CIMARRON
⟨Beverly Hills⟩

"CIMARRON" is a grill dish restaurant whose name derives from a New Mexican valley and whose dishes and design introduce a Southwestern taste.
Situated on the 1st floor of "The Village," a shopping center in Beverly Hills, the restaurant is totally finished in a Western motif. Hand-made barstools have been installed on the bar corner representing an old stable, and the wall is decorated with wall ornaments made by Indians.
The owner-chef, Jim Lynn Jr. offers, unique foods with a light and healthy taste using herbs and spices.
＜CIMARRON＞
Number of guest seats/165 (dining 90, courtyard 45, bar 30)
Address/301 N. Canon Drive Beverly Hills, CA 90210
Phone/213-278-2277

店名はニューメキシコ地方の渓谷の名に由来し 料理や店舗デザインにサウスウエスタンのテイストがいかされたグリル料理レストラン。
ビバリーヒルズのショッピングセンター The Village の1階にあるこの店は ウエスタンのモチーフで統一されている。 古い馬小屋をイメージしたバーコーナーにはハンドメイドのバースツールが置かれ 壁面にはインディアンが作った壁飾りがディスプレイされている。
ハーブやスパイスを使ったライトでヘルシーな味付けで オーナー シェフのジム リン Jr(Jim Lynn,Jr.) は独自の料理を提供している。
〈シマロン〉
客席数/165席(ダイニング 90席 コートヤード席 45席 バー 30席)
Address/301 N.Canon Drive Bevery Hills, CA 90210
Phone/213-278-2277

1/The entrance area; designed to have a Southwestern atmosphere.
2/The bar corner.
3/The facade; situated on the central court yard of a shopping center.
4/A very impressive toilet.

1/エントランス廻りをみる　サウス ウエスタンの雰囲気でまとめている
2/バーコーナーをみる
3/ファサード　ショピングセンターの中央コートヤードにある
4/強烈な印象をあたえる洗面室

⑤

⑥

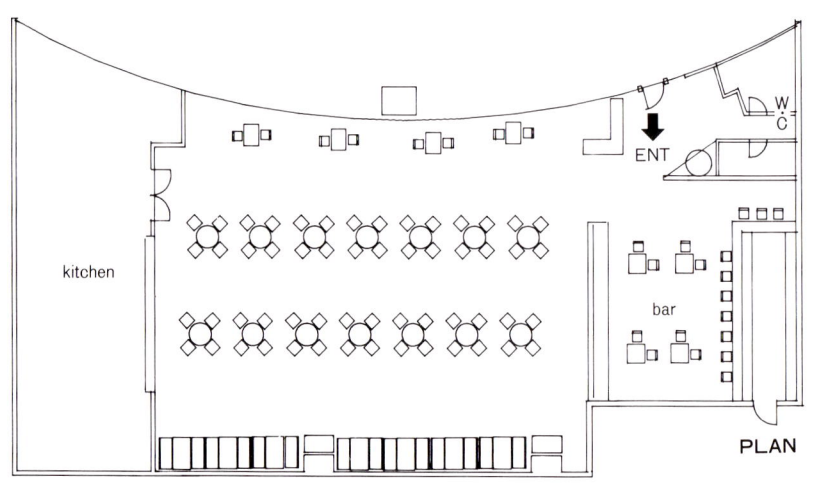

PLAN

⑦

ⓐ

ⓑ

●menu
a : LOBSTER WITH A SPICY SHRIMP SAUCE.
b : SALMON TARTARE CURED IN
    CILANTRO & GOLD TEQUILA.
c : MESQUITE GRILLED VEAL CHOP
    RUBBED WITH ROSEMARY & GARLIC.

5/The open dining room; the courtyard is visible.
6/The booth seating area with a Western atmosphere.
7/The owner-chef Jim Lynn Jr. says: "Taste, like color, is produced from various combinations."

5/コートヤードが眺められる開放的なダイニングルーム
6/ウエスタンの雰囲気を醸し出すブース席
7/オーナー シェフの Jim Lynn Jr. は"味とは 色と同様にさまざまなコンビネーションによって生み出される"と語る

ⓒ

GORDON BIERSCH
⟨San Francisco⟩

This is a brewery restaurant equipped with a beer brewery which opened on the former site of a coffee factory facing the San Francisco Bay. It serves home-made beer brewed by using a German computer-controlled brewing machine into which carefully selected hops, aroma and yeast are added.

With beer as the staple beverage, the menu is mainly composed of an eclectic collection of cuisines such as Southwestern, Mediterranean, Asian and German, which are prepared in a lively open kitchen.

The interior space is composed of the 1st floor beer hall and 2nd floor restaurant, and features a strange harmony between the inorganic atmosphere of a brick wall, a concrete floor and steel pipes running through the pillars and the gentle, warm atmosphere of the mahogany counter and lighting. The pleasingly cool sound of jazz as BGM is playing.

<GORDON BIERSCH>
Number of guest seats/360 (restaurant 190, beer hall 170)
Address/2 Harrison Street San Francisco, CA 94105
Phone/415-243-8246

サンフランシスコ湾に面したコーヒー工場跡にオープンした ビール醸造所をもつブリュワリーレストラン。ホップ アロマ イーストなど厳選された素材を コンピュータ管理されたドイツ製の醸造機でホームメイドされたビールを提供している。料理はビールに合わせ サウスウエスタン 地中海風 アジア料理 ドイツ料理など エクレクティックなメニューが中心で 臨場感あふれるオープンキッチンで調理されている。店内は 1階のビヤホールと2階のレストランで構成され 煉瓦の壁面 コンクリートのフロア 柱の間を縫って走るスチールパイプの無機的な雰囲気と マホガニーのカウンターや照明の柔らかく暖かい感じが うまく調和している。ＢＧＭのクールなジャズのサウンドが心地良い。

〈ゴードン ビアーシュ〉
客席数/360席(レストラン 190席 ビヤホール 170席)
Address/2 Harrison Street San Francisco, CA 94105
Phone/415-243-8246

1/The beer hall on the 1st floor; the restaurant is on the 2nd floor. The mahogany counter is equipped with delivery tubs for three types of beer brewed at this shop.
2/The facade; with a simple sign which stands out well.
3/The 1st floor beer hall viewed from the 2nd floor restaurant through the stairwell.

1/1階 ビヤホール 2階がレストラン マホガニーのカウンターには この店で醸造される3種のビールの取り出しタブが設けられている
2/ファサード シンプルなサインがよく目立つ
3/2階レストランと吹き抜けを通して 1階ビヤホールをみる

③

open kitchen
ENT
E.V.
1F PLAN

open kitchen
reception
stair well
stair well
beer tank
E.V.
2F PLAN

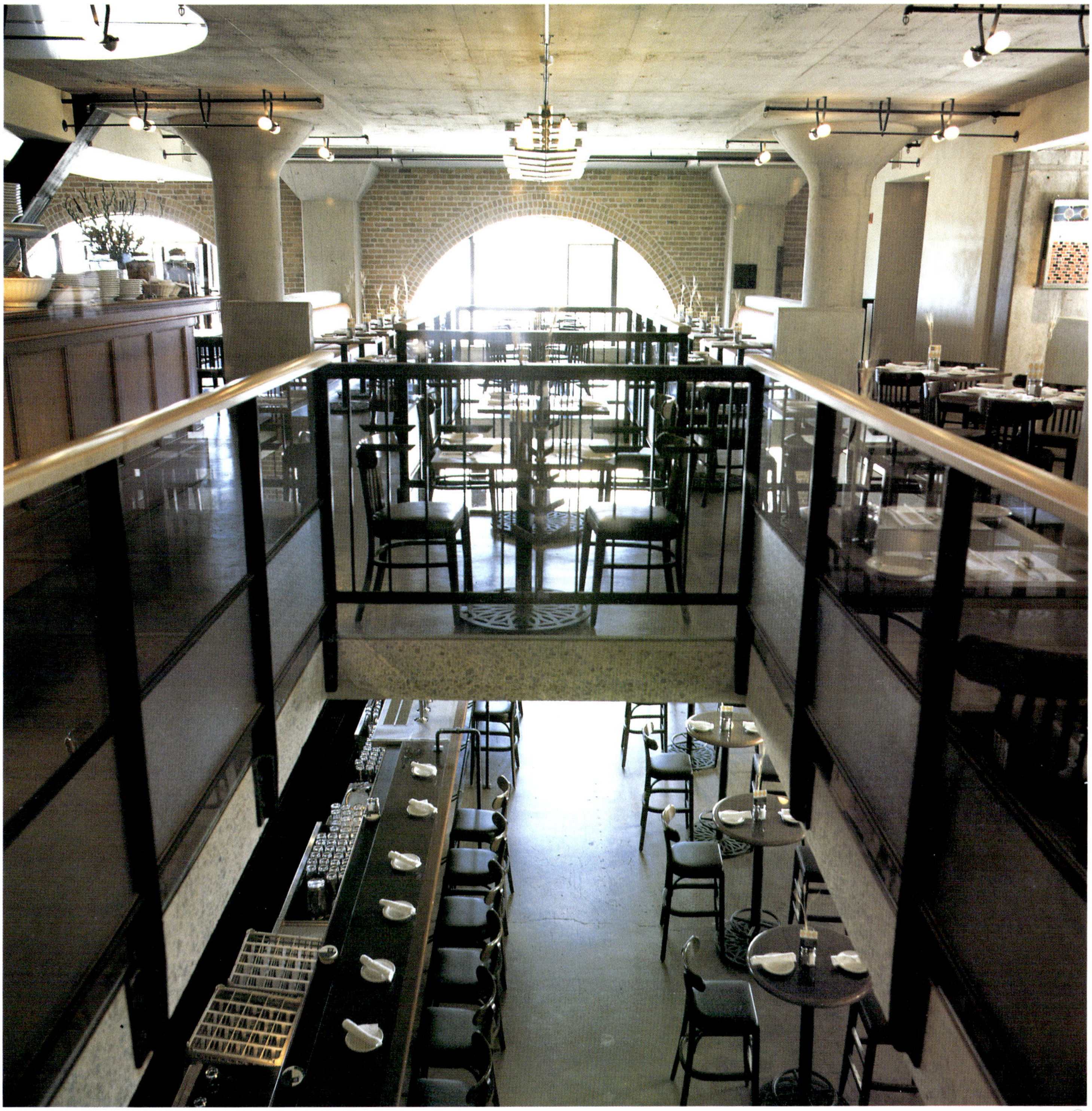

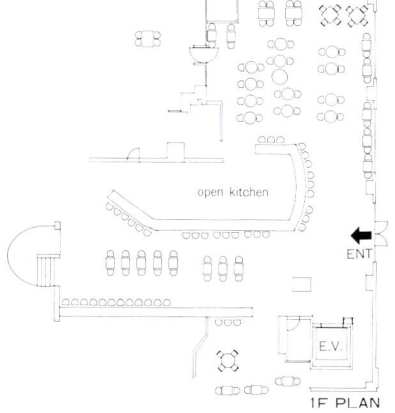

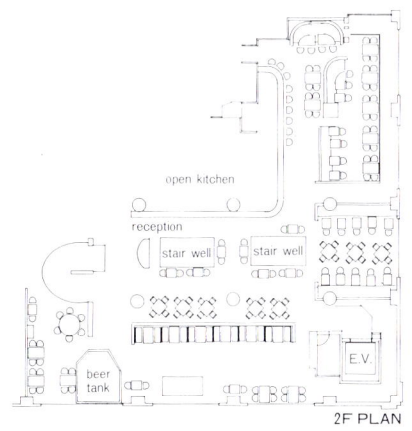

④

⑤

⑥

4/The 1st floor counter seating area; beer brewing processes visible behind the glass.
5/A beer tank in the 2nd floor restaurant; forming part of the interior.
6/Dean Biersch (left), one of the owners, and the chef Ilana Saraf.

4/1階 カウンター席 ガラスの向こうにビールの醸造過程を見せている
5/2階 レストランのビヤタンク インテリアになっている
6/オーナーの一人 Dean Biersch（左）とシェフの Ilana Saraf

● menu
a : BARBEQUED PORK SANDWICH, ON HOUSE MADE KAISER ROLL WITH ONION STRINGS + TRI-COLOR SLAW.
b : TUNA SASHIMI AND HOUSE CURED SALMON / stacked on fried wonton skins with pickled cucumber and daikon in a soy-wasabi-sherry vinaigrette.
c : PENNE PASTA / with browned garlic, sauteed peppers, onions greens and fresh tomato in a warm balsamic vinaigrette with Parmesano Reggiano.

CHILLERS
⟨Santa Monica⟩

This restaurant, which opened before the Third Street Promenade as a result of Santa Monica redevelopment project, features 22 types of frozen cocktail having unique names, such as the apparently awful "Nitrogrycerin," "Summer Heat" which reminds us of the intensely hot midsummer sun, and "Pink Panty" which is a little sexy. As new tools, colorful dispensers have been installed in front of the inner bar counter, and employees in casual uniform quite becoming to Santa Monica fill a hard cup with vividly colored cocktail. A patio installed on the colorful dining area is very impressive.
<CHILLERS>
Number of guest seats/230
Address/1446 Third Street Promenade Santa Monica, CA 90401
Phone/213-394-1933

サンタモニカの再開発計画でサード ストリートのプロムナードに面してオープンしたこのレストランの売り物は 22種類のフローズンカクテルでそれぞれユニークな名前がつけられている。例えばいかにも恐ろしい "ニトログリセリン" とか 真夏の強烈な太陽を思わせる "サマーヒート" ちょっとセクシーな "ピンクパンティ" など……ユニークなネーミングである。店内奥のバーカウンターの前に並ぶカラフルなディスペンサーが新兵器で いかにもサンタモニカらしいカジュアルなユニフォームの従業員が 鮮やかな色のカクテルをハードカップに満たしてくれる。カラフルなダイニングに併設されたパティオが特徴的である。
〈チラーズ〉
客席数/230席
Address/1446 Third Street Promenade Santa Monica, CA 90401
Phone/213-394-1933

①

1/ The facade with a patio seating space.
2/ The bar lounge in the center; high tables and stools are exposed to natural light from the ceiling.
3/ The dining and inner areas viewed from the entrance.
4/ The dining area.

1/パティオ席のあるファサード
2/店内中央のバーラウンジ 高いテーブルとスツールが天井からの自然光に照らされている
3/エントランスからダイニングエリアと奥をみる
4/ダイニングエリアをみる

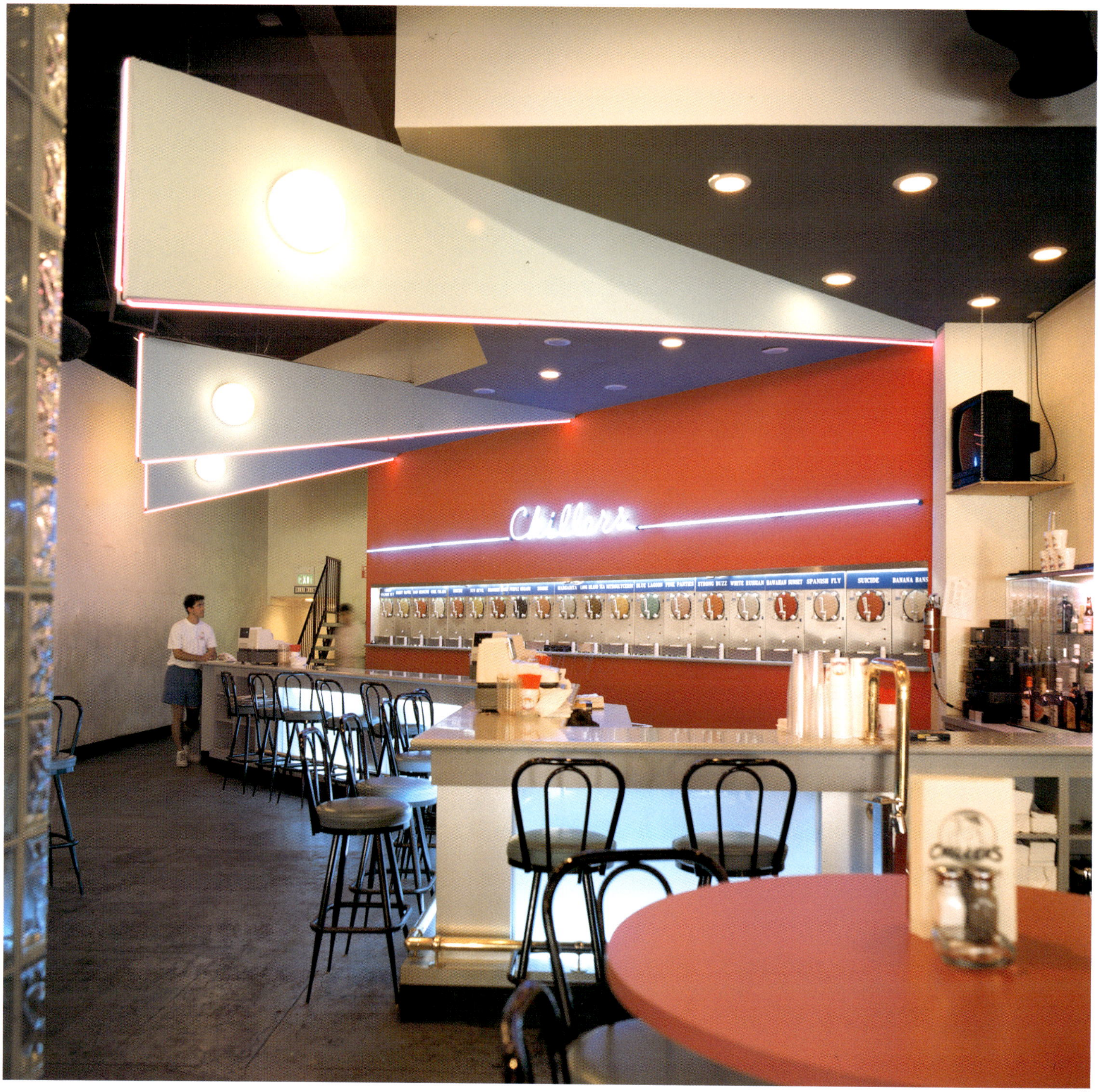
Chillers
SUICIDE
SPANISH FLY

⑤

Chillers
SUICIDE
SPANISH FLY
WHITE RUSSIAN

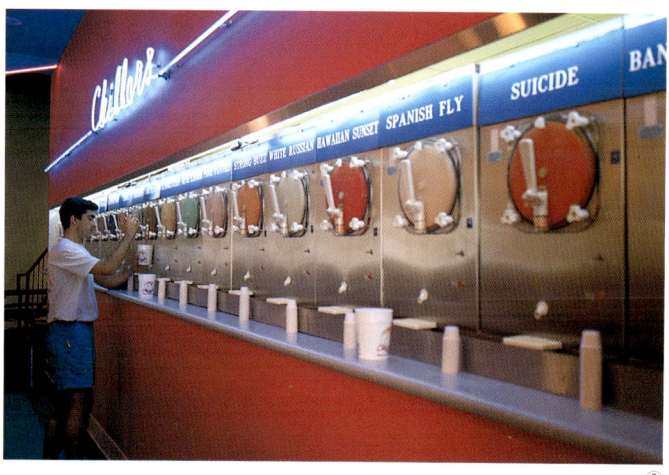

⑥

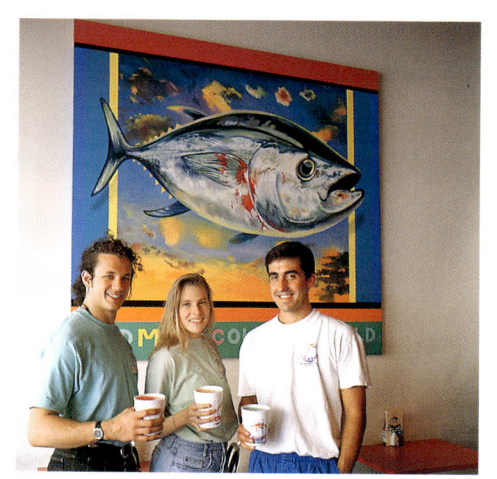

⑦

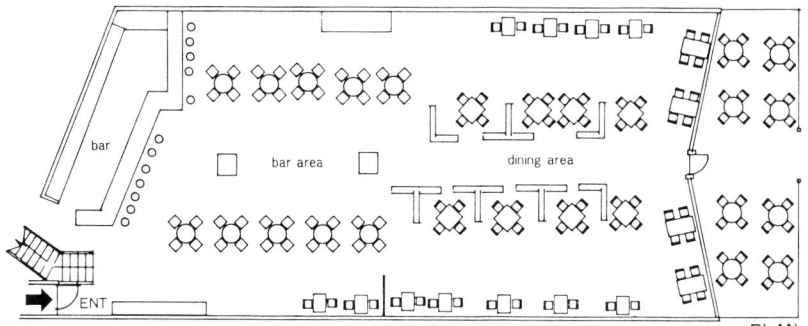

5/ The inner bar corner; composed of frozen cocktail and full bar service counters.
6·8/ The colorful bar counter; various types of frozen cocktail having unique names are displayed. Small cups are for tasting.
7/ T-shirt with a logomark is uniform.

5/店内奥 バーコーナー フローズンカクテルとフルバーのサービスカウンターで構成されている
6·8/カラフルなバーカウンター ユニークなネーミングのフローズンカクテルが並ぶ 小さなカップはテイスティング用
7/ロゴマーク入りのTシャツがユニフォーム

PARAGON BAR & CAFE
⟨San Francisco⟩

This is a long established shop which has been patronized by community inhabitants as a cafe & bar where jazz and blues performance can be enjoyed. Since the opening in the 1930s, it has changed hands and was renovated at the end of 1991. The interior design was undertaken by David Berman and Ron Nunn, while the wall design was undertaken by Michael Brennan.
The atmosphere of a 1938 tavern has been skillfully preserved including the facade, sign and interior, in order to utilize a time-honored artistic sense.
Metal sculptures were produced by Mark Bulwinkle and wall paintings in the dining area by Heather Wilcox. Thus, these artists collaborated to create a shop which features a harmonious contrast of modern and traditional elements.
The foods cooked by the chef Kerry Heffernan are so simple and familiar that the title "American bistro foods" may suit them exactly. The day-by-day menu is also popular.
<PARAGON BAR & CAFE>
Number of guest seats/72 (dining 42, bar 30)
Address/3251 Scott Street San Francisco, CA 94123
Phone/415-922-2456

ジャズとブルースの演奏が聞かれるカフェ&バーとして 地元の人たちに親しまれている歴史のある店。1930年代に開店以来 何度か代が変り'91年暮にリニューアルしたもので デザインは David Berman と Ron Nunn 壁面のデザインは Michael Brennanが担当した。
1938年代当時のタバーンの雰囲気をファサード サイン インテリアにいたるまでうまく残し 時間を経た芸術的な感覚を活かしてる。
メタル作品は Mark Bulwinkle ダイニングエリアの壁画は Heather Wilcox で これらのアーティストたちの合作で モダンと伝統がマッチしたコントラストのある店舗づくりになっている。
シェフ Kerry Heffernan の料理はアメリカンビストロ料理とでも表現できるシンプルで親しみのあるもので 日変わりメニューもあって好評である。
〈パラゴン バー&カフェ〉
客席数/72席（ダイニング 42席 バー 30席）
Address/3251 Scott Street San Francisco, CA 94123
Phone/415-922-2456

1/ The bar area; designed to give a time-honored atmosphere.
2/ The dining area viewed from the bar area.
3/ The signboard put up at the time of opening in 1938 is used without any change.
4/ The dining area viewed across an old fireplace and stage (left).

1/バーエリアをみる 歴史を感じさせる雰囲気づくりをしている
2/バーエリアからダイニングエリアをみる
3/1938年の開店時のサインボードをそのまま使用している
4/古い暖炉とステージ(左)越しにダイニングをみる

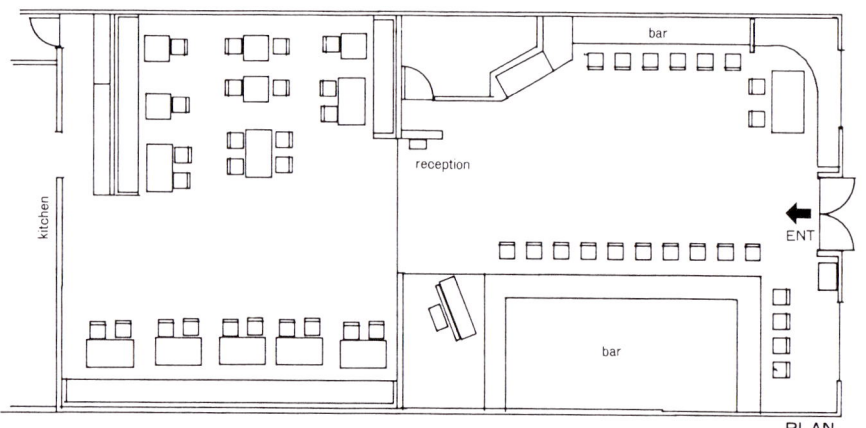

PLAN

5/The dining room; with Heather Wilcox's rhythmical wall painting.
6/The bar counter; accented with the wall painting as reflected in the mirror at the back.
7/The chef Kerry Heffernan; developing American bistro foods.

5/ダイニングルーム　リズミカルな壁画は Heather Wilcox の作品
6/バーカウンター　背後のミラーに壁面のアートが映りこんでいる
7/シェフ Kerry Heffernan　アメリカン ビストロ料理を開発している

● menu
a : SEARED RARE AHI TUNA SANDWICH / with lemon aioli and a tomato basil salad.
b : GRILLED RIBEYE STEAK / with griddle cooked garlic potatoes and apple-parsley chutney.
c : CHOCOLATE, WALNUT BRROWNIE WITH FRESH STRAWBERRIES AND VANILLA ICE CREAM.

JOHNNY LOVE'S
⟨San Francisco⟩

This bar & grill that is the hottest night spot in San Francisco. The interior space is composed of a bar area, dining area with a stage, and an open kitchen accented with wine colored walls, green leather stools and booths. The floor of the bar area is finished with concrete tiles, while that of the dining room is wooden. From 10:00 p.m. only the booths are operated, while the other areas become a dance floor, so that the interior space as a whole changes into a night club.

The shop name comes from Johnny "Love" Metheny, who is one of the owners and a popular local bartender whose fans come to meet him. The menu is composed of Southwestern eclectic foods cooked by Mark "Spike" Hartman.

Since there is no other restaurant with a dance floor on the North Market Street, "JOHNNY LOVE'S" is crowded everyday, and two bands perform blues, reggae, rockabilly, rock 'n' roll, etc.

⟨JOHNNY LOVE'S⟩
Number of guest seats/120 (dining 80, bar 40)
Address/1500 Broadway at Polk St. San Francisco, CA
Phone/415-931-6053

サンフランシスコでもっともホットなナイトスポットのバー&グリル。店内はバーエリア　ステージがあるダイニングエリア　オープンキッチンなどで構成され　ワインカラーの壁面とグリーンのレザー張りのスツールやブースなどでアクセントをつけている。床はバーエリアがコンクリートタイル　ダイニングが木製になっている。夜10時からはレストランはブースのみの営業で　他はダンスフロアになり　店全体がナイトクラブの様相に変る。オーナーの一人で　店名にもなっている　ジョニィ"ラブ"メセニィ（Johnny "Love" Metheny）は　地元の人気バーテンダーで　彼のファンが集まってくる。料理は　Mark "Spike" Hartman のサウスウエスタン調のエクレクティック料理。

ノース　マーケットストリート地区にはダンスフロアを持つレストランがないので　連日賑わいをみせ　2つのバンドがブルース　レゲエ　ロカビリィ　ロックンロールなどを演奏している。

〈ジョニー　ラブス〉
客席数/120席（ダイニング　80席　バー　40席）
Address/1500 Broadway at Polk St.San Francisco,CA
Phone/415-931-6053

①

1/ The reception area and bar corner.
2/ The bar counter and dining area viewed from the entrance hall.
3/ The facade.
4/ The bar corner.

1/レセプションとバーコーナーをみる
2/エントランスホールからバーカウンターとダイニングをみる
3/ファサード
4/バーコーナーをみる

5/ The open kitchen behind the booth seating area; with a showy artwork on the upper wall.
6/ The dining area viewed from the stage; at 10:00 p.m. this space changes into a dance floor in only 3 or 4 minutes.
7/ The owner Johnny "Love" Metheny; he is also a popular host.

5/ブース席後方のオープンキッチン 上部壁面のアートワークが目立つ
6/ステージ上からダイニングをみる 夜の10時にはこのスペースが3〜4分でダンスフロアに変わる
7/オーナー Johnny "Love" Metheny は人気のホストでもある

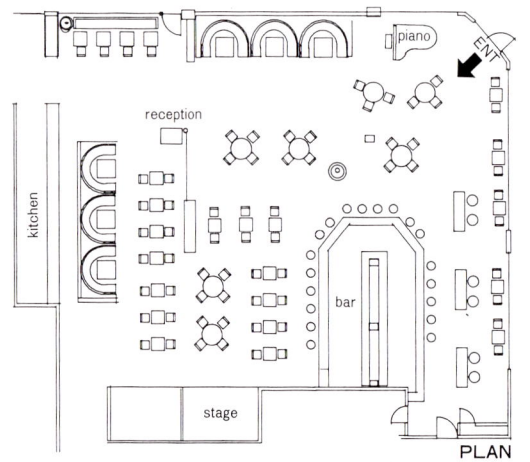

PLAN

● menu
a : GRILLED BONELESS CHICKEN BREAST / with creamy polenta, wild mushrooms and sage aioli.
b : POACHED SEA SCALLOPS & EGG FETTUCINE / with roast peppers and Italian parsley pesto.
c : PAN SEARED LOCAL HALIBUT / with creamed corn and red bell pepper sauce.

LAWRY'S THE PRIME RIB
⟨Beverly Hills⟩

This is a new restaurant opened by a roast beef restaurant which opened in 1983, on the occasion of their 55th anniversary. Facing La Cienega Blvd., it is a spacious restaurant having 450 seats, and composed of dining, bar and lounge areas. The interior is designed with an image like a British membership club.
By weighing the restaurant's own tradition, not merely the interior but also foods and services are arranged to retain the original elements which have existed since their opening in 1938 so that guests do not feel any change in the interior. Guests are strongly impressed with the refined and attentive services.
<LAWRY'S THE PRIME RIB>
Number of guest seats/450
Address/100 North La Cienega Blvd. Beverly Hills, CA 90211
Phone/310-652-2827

1938年に開店したローストビーフの専門レストランが 創業55年を機に新館をオープンした。ラ シエネガ通り(La Cienega Blvd.)に面したレストランは 450席と広く ダイニング バー ラウンジで構成され インテリアはイギリスの会員制クラブのイメージでまとめられている。
レストランの伝統を重視し インテリアのみでなく 料理やサービスに至るまで 開店時と同じように 客に変化を全く感じさせないように心掛けているという。洗練され 手慣れたサービスは訪れた人たちに強い印象を与えている。
〈ローリース ザ プライム リブ〉
客席数/450席
Address/100 North La Cienega Blvd. Beverly Hills, CA 90211
Phone/310-652-2827

②

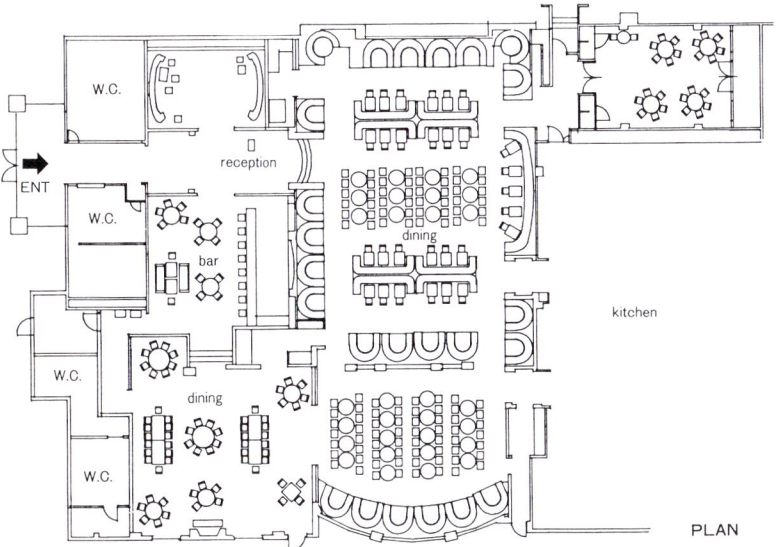

1/The reception area viewed from the entrance hall.
2/The main dining area; with large impressive paintings.

PLAN

1/エントランスホールからレセプション方向をみる
2/メインダイニング　大きな壁画が印象的である

3/The bar corner.
4/The lounge; gives an image of an English saloon.
5/The dining area features an atmosphere like that of a British membership club.
6/An oval room; the wall is decorated with various types of frames.
7/A VIP room decorated with wall paintings of winery; with an inner wine cellar which stocks 4,000 bottles.
8/The facade and signboard.

3/バーコーナー
4/ラウンジ イギリスのサルーンをイメージさせる
5/暖炉のあるダイニングはイギリスの会員制クラブの雰囲気
6/オーバル ルーム 楕円形で壁面にはいろいろな形の額が飾られている
7/VIPルーム ワイナリーを描いた壁画が飾られ 奥は4000本をストックするワインセラーになっている
8/ファサードとサインボード

LUNARIA
⟨Los Angeles⟩

A modern French/Californian food bistro being managed by the owner Bernard Jacoupy and the chef Dominique Chavanon who were born in France. The shop name "LUNARIA" comes from the fact that the owner's grandfather was fond of lunaria.
Composed of dining, oyster bar, jazz lounge, benquet and other areas, the interior space looks like a gallery, as it it decorated with 120 pictures painted by the grandfather who was an impressionist. While featuring modern elements, the restaurant serves foods at reasonable prices in a casual and homey atmosphere.
Compared to Beverly Hills and Century City where many high-class restaurants are operating, this modern bistro is favorably accepted.
<LUNARIA>
Number of guest seats/280 (dining 100, lounge 40, oyster bar 20, banquet room 120)
Address/10351 Santa Monica Blvd. Los Angeles, CA 90025
Phone/213-282-8870

フランス生まれのオーナー ベルナルド ジャコピー(Bernard Jacoupy)とシェフ ドミニク シャバノン(Dominique Chavanon)が経営するモダーン フレンチ/カリフォルニア料理のビストロ。店名の「ルナーリア(月見草)」はオーナーの祖父が好きだったことに由来する。
ダイニング オイスターバー ジャズ ラウンジ 宴会場などで構成される店内には 印象派の画家だった祖父の作品が 120枚も飾られギャラリーのような店造りで モダーンを強調しながらも カジュアルで親しみやすい雰囲気の中でリーズナブルな価格で料理を提供している。
高級レストランの多いビバリーヒルズやセンチュリーシティを背景にモダーンなビストロの登場が話題になっている。
〈ルナーリア〉
客席数/280席(ダイニング 100席 ラウンジ 40席 オイスターバー 20席 バンケットルーム 120席)
Address/10351 Santa Monica Blvd. Los Angeles, CA 90025
Phone/213-282-8870

①

1/The entrance area viewed from an aisle to the bar; the aisle is gently sloped.
2/The dining room.
3/The entrance.
4/The bar area viewed from the sunroom/dining space.

1/バーへの通路からエントランス方向をみる 通路はゆるやかなスロープがつけられている
2/ダイニングルームをみる
3/エントランス
4/サンルームのダイニングよりバー方向をみる

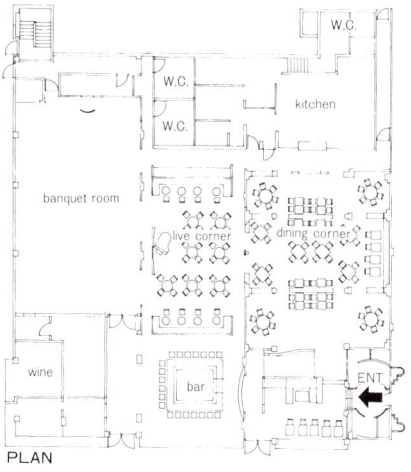

5/The oyster bar; designed in an Italian style.
6/The jazz lounge viewed from the dining area; with the slide panel wall which can be opened/closed.

5/オイスターバー　イタリア調にまとめている
6/ダイニングからジャズラウンジをみる　壁面はスライド式パネルで開閉が可能

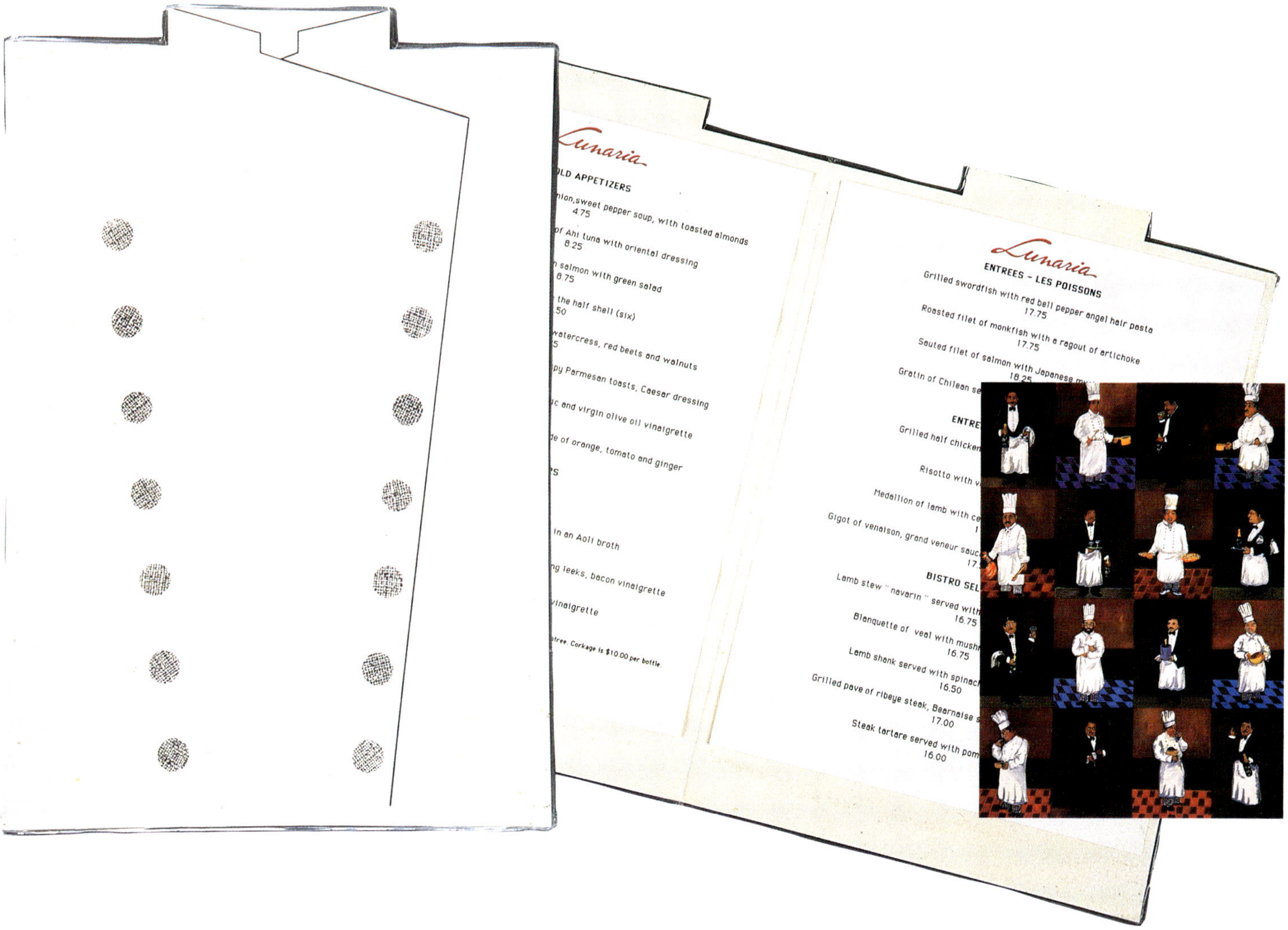

● menu
a : LAMB SHANK SERVED WITH SPINACH AND A CURRY SAUCE.
b : SAUTEED FILET OF SALMON WITH JAPANESE MUSHROOM.

RÖCKENWAGNER
⟨Santa Monica⟩

This restaurant is situated on a corner of the commercial composite facility "Edgemar" which appeared on the former site of a dairy house as a result of redevelopment. The corner is composed of a bookstore, gallery, gift shop, art museum, etc. The owner Röckenwagner uses his own name as his shop name. He is also known as the owner of "FAMA" (see page 102) which was designed by David Kellen who also designed this restaurant.
"RÖCKENWAGNER" is a bistro-type shop having a bakery, and a high-ceiled interior space, which looks like a loft, is bright with natural light coming in, and designed to have a composed atmosphere by using wood and bricks.
In addition to Californian cuisine, French foods arranged with German elements are served here. Generally characterized by moderate butter and cream, and voluminous vegetables.
＜RÖCKENWAGNER＞
Number of guest seats/75
Address/2435 Main Street Santa Monica, CA 90405
Phone/310-399-6504

ミルク工場の跡地に再開発された複合商業施設 「エッジマー (Edgemar)」内の書店 ギャラリー ギフトショップ 美術館などで構成される一角にある。店名はオーナーの名前をそのままとったもの。レッケンバグナー（Rökenwagner）は「FAMA」（本書 102ページ収録）のオーナーとしても知られ デザインも同じ David Kellen。
このレストランは ベーカリーをもつビストロタイプの店で 天井の高いロフト感覚の店内は自然光を採りいれ明るく 木と煉瓦で落ち着きのあるデザインでまとめられている。料理はコンテンポラリーなカリフォルニア料理と ドイツ風のアレンジをしたフランス料理で バターやクリームの量を控え 野菜類を多く付け合わせているのが特徴。
〈レッケンバグナー〉
客席数/75席
Address/2435 Main Street Santa Monica, CA 90405
Phone/310-399-6504

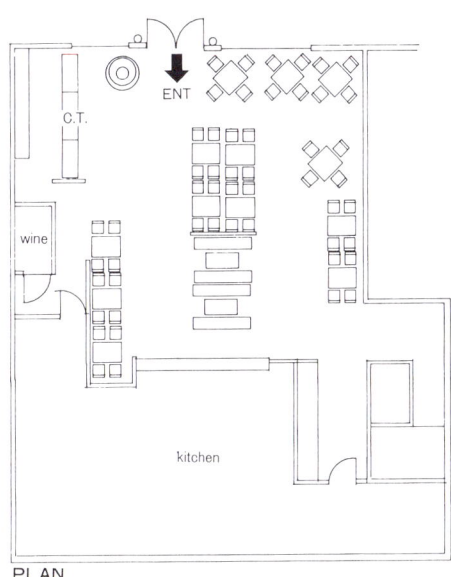

②

③

1/The facade facing the courtyard of "Edgemar Complex."
2/A design of the dining area featuring a combination of wooden elements.
3/A selling corner of bakery near the entrance.

1/Edgemar Complex の中庭に面したファサード
2/木を組み合わせたダイニングのデザイン
3/エントランス近くのベーカリーの販売コーナー

● menu
a : SHORT STACK of smoked wild scottish salmon, potato chips, creme fraiche and caviar.
b : PORK TENDERLOIN rolled in cracked pepper and topped with goat cheese, with roasted peppers and spaetzle.
c : LOBSTER MEDALLIONS WITH CORNUCOPIA OF ASPARAGUS and sweet and sour balsamico sauce.

4/The dining area extending under the high ceiling like a warehouse; gives an open sense as if the wall paintings are continuing to the outside.

4/倉庫のイメージで 高い天井空間に広がるダイニング 壁画がそのまま外に続いているようなオープンな感じを与えている

MICHAEL'S WATERSIDE
⟨Santa Barbara⟩

Situated about 100 miles (160 km) north of Los Angeles, Santa Barbara, home to this restaurant, is blessed with marine and farm products.
Since the opening, the owner-chef, Michael Hatchings, has continued to attract many people by offering foods cooked by using fresh and ample ingredients. He has accumulated a lot of experience in the kitchens of famous French restaurants in the U.S.A. and in Europe, and sticks to materials more than anyone else. He is also engaged in the culture of mushrooms and abalone.
A Victorian private house built in 1872 was renovated to create this restaurant. Built in the French provincial style, this restaurant is highly reputed for its elegant and homely atmosphere, and has been often featured in the media.
＜MICHAEL'S WATERSIDE＞
Number of guest seats/110
Address/50 Los Patos Way Santa Barbara, CA 93108
Phone/805-969-0307

サンタバーバラはロサンゼルスから北へ約100マイル（160km） 太平洋をのぞむ 海や山の幸に恵まれたところ。
オーナー シェフのマイケル ハッチング（Michael Hatchings）は その豊富で新鮮な素材を活かした料理を提供し 開店以来多くの人たちを魅了し続けている。アメリカやヨーロッパの有名なフランス料理店のキッチンで豊富な経験を積んだ彼の 素材へのこだわりは人一倍で ワイルドマッシュルームの栽培やアワビなどの養殖もてがけている。
1872年に建てられたビクトリア調の民家をリニューアルしたこのレストランは フランスの田舎風の造りで エレガントで家庭的な雰囲気が好評でマスコミでもたびたび紹介されている。
〈マイケルズ ウォーターサイド〉
客席数/110席
Address/50 Los Patos Way Santa Barbara, CA 93108
Phone/805-969-0307

1/The facade; renovated from a private house built in 1872.
2/The dining room.
3/The reception in the entrance hall.
4/The dining area near the entrance; changes into a private room when sliding the wooden door.

1/ファサード 1872年に建てられた民家をリニューアル
2/ダイニングルーム
3/エントランスホール廻り レセプションをみる
4/エントランスそばのダイニング 木製のドアをスライドさせると個室になる

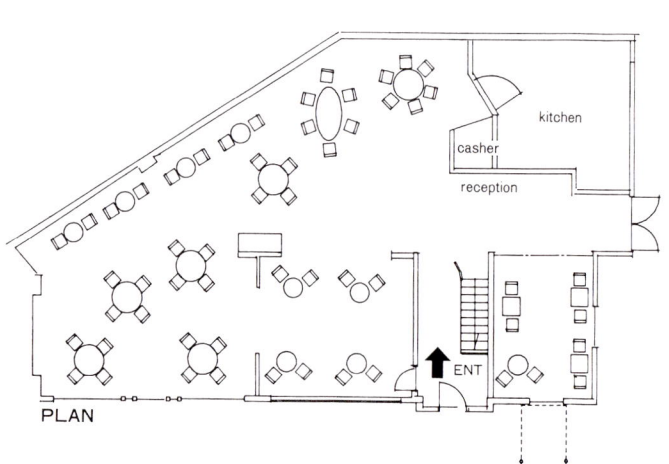

(a)

(b)

5/ Natural light comes in the dining room having a homely atmosphere; accented with wine colored chairs and napkins.
6/ The wall decorated with flower paintings; using the mirror effectively.
7/ A view from the window is reputed together with the owner-chef Michael Hutchings.

5/家庭的な雰囲気のダイニングルームには自然光が射しこみ ワインカラーの椅子やナプキンがアクセントになっている
6/花の絵画が飾られた壁面　ミラーが効果的に使用されている
7/窓からの眺めも　オーナー　シェフ Michael Hutchings とともに知られている

⑦

●menu
a : BABY ABALONE WITH A DILL SAUCE.
b : BAKED SALMON "PERSILLADE" ON ORIENTAL VEGETABLES.

AQUA
⟨San Francisco⟩

An upscale seafood restaurant whose name "Aqua" means water in Latin. Situated on a financial quarter in downtown San Francisco, it is managed by Mr. & Mrs. Morrone. A bank building has been renovated into this restaurant whose high-ceiled bright interior space is composed of a bar corner using maple and a dining area having a cream & peach wall which is accented with large mirrors. The sophisticated interior design was undertaken by local artists Wendy Tsuji and Frank Frost.
The owner-chef George Morrone is particular about fish as to their places of origin and also organically cultured vegetables, since he is always intent on offering creative fish foods. His wife Stacey mainly undertakes front and accounting duties.
<AQUA>
Number of guest seats/121 (dining 105, bar 16)
Address/252 California Street San Francisco, CA 94111
Phone/415-956-9662

ラテン語で"水"という店名のアップスケールのシーフードレストラン。モローン (Morrone) 夫妻の経営で サンフランシスコのダウンタウン 金融街に立地している。銀行の建物のリニューアルで 高い天井の明るい空間でメープル材を使用したバーコーナー とクリーム ピーチ色の壁面に大きなミラーを配したダイニングエリアで構成されている。
ソフィスティケイトされた店内のデザインは地元のアーティスト Wendy Tsuji と Frank Frost。
オーナー シェフのジョージ モローン (George Morrone) は 魚介類の産地や有機野菜にこだわり クリエイティブな魚料理を手掛けている。
奥さんのステイシー (Stacey) は主にフロントと経理を担当している。
〈アクア〉
客席数/121席（ダイニング 105席　バー 16席）
Address/252 California Street San Francisco, CA 94111
Phone/415-956-9662

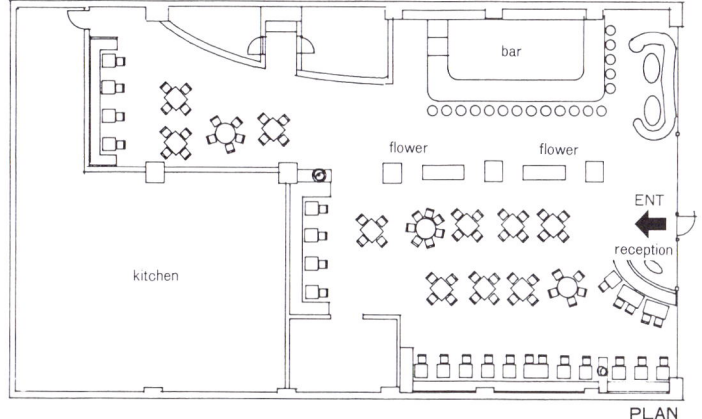

PLAN

1/The entrance hall.
2/The dining room; with a large mirror set in the wall looking like a frame.

1/エントランスホールをみる
2/ダイニングルーム　壁面にはめ込まれた大きなミラーが額縁のよう

3/The bar counter; finished with natural colors using maple.
4/The bar area composed of high-ceiled space and stone floor.
5/The ironwork reception desk.
6/The owners George & Stacey Morrone.

3/バーカウンター メープル材を使用し自然色でまとめている
4/高い天井空間と石のフロアで構成されたバーエリア
5/アイアンワークのレセプションデスク
6/オーナーの George & Stacey Morrone 夫妻

(a)

(b)

(6)

(c)

● menu
a : SEARED SCALLOP AND FOIE GRAS SALAD / Belgian Endive, Carmelized Rhubarb-Lime compote.
b : CHESAPEAKE BAY SOFT SHELL CRABS / Tempura Battered, Curry Vinaigrette.
c : CHILLED FRUIT COMPOTES WITH RESPECTIVE SORBETS / Red Currant, Pineapple, Blackberry.

ONE MARKET RESTAURANT
⟨San Francisco⟩

This restaurant serves American home foods cooked by mainly using locally available ingredients. It is jointly managed by the chef Bradley Ogden and consultant Michael Dellar. It opened on the 1st floor of the Southern Pacific Building which was constructed in 1917 on the point where Market Street, San Francisco, starts. Passersby can look into the restaurant which looks like a casual American bistro. It is designed by Jim Maxwell and Cindy Beckman at the advice of color consultant Jill Pileroscia.

Under the high ceiling, pieces of white tablecloth lie vividly in a row, accented with purple on the pillars and chairs. The interior space features a composed atmosphere with the marble table top in the bar corner and the floor covered over with natural stone. An oven using firewood at the back of the dining area and an inner kitchen give an open impression, and it is amusing to view busily working cooks.

The restaurant is fully operating all day long from breakfast to lunch and dinner, as well as for snack and takeout services.

<ONE MARKET RESTAURANT>
Number of guest seats/258 (dining 170, bar 44, private room 44)
Address/1 Market Street San Francisco, CA 94015-1572
Phone/415-777-5577

ローカルでとれた食材をメインにしたアメリカの家庭料理を提供するレストラン。シェフの Bradley Ogden とコンサルタント Michael Dellar の共同経営で サンフランシスコのマーケットストリートが始まる最初の地点に1917年に建造された サザーン パシフィックビルの1階にオープンした。外から店内が眺められ カジュアルなアメリカンビストロといった雰囲気。デザインは Jim Maxwell と Cindy Beckman で カラーコンサルタントは Jill Pileroscia。

高い天井の下に並ぶ白いテーブルクロスが鮮やかで 柱と椅子のパープルがアクセントをつけている。バーコーナーのマーブルのテーブルトップや自然石を貼りつめたフロアが落ち着きを感じさせる。ダイニングエリアの奥の薪用のオーブンや 後方のキッチンがオープンな感じで 忙しく立ち働くコックたちを見るのも楽しい。

朝食 ランチ ディナー バー スナック テイクアウトなど 一日中フル稼動のレストランである。

⟨ワン マーケット レストラン⟩
客席数/258席(ダイニング 170席 バー 44席 個室 44席)
Address/1 Market Street San Francisco, CA 94015-1572
Phone/415-777-5577

1/The bar viewed from the entrance hall.
2/The dining room; the window portion is in the stairwell along the opening.

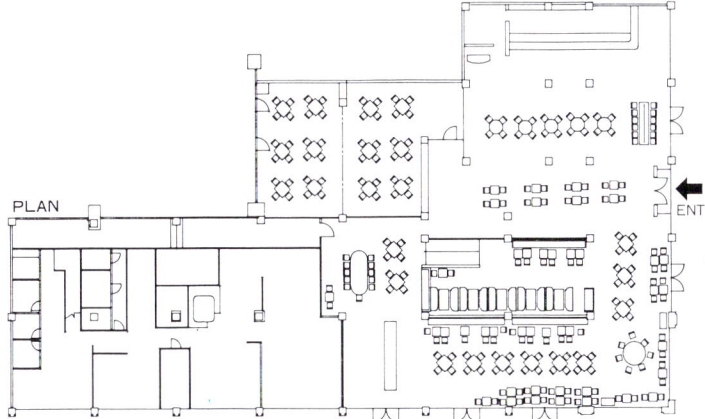

1/エントランスホールからバーをみる
2/ダイニングルーム　窓の部分は開口部に沿って吹き抜けになっている

③

④

⑤

⑥

⑦

3/The display kitchen at an inner part of the dining area.
4/The facade/entrance.
5/The kitchen facing the pavement.
6/The open kitchen is such that it looks like a part of the dining room.
7/The owner Michael Dellar and chef-owner Bradley Ogden.

3/ダイニングエリアの後方のディスプレイキッチンをみる
4/ファサード エントランスをみる
5/歩道に面したキッチンをみる
6/ダイニングの一部の様なオープンキッチン
7/オーナー Michael Dellar と シェフ オーナー Bradley Ogden

161

ELKA
⟨San Francisco⟩

This seafood restaurant serves as the main dining space of the "Miyako Hotel" in San Francisco. The shop name comes from Elka Gilmore, general chef of this restaurant. It opened with the support of the Miyako Hotel which is intent on "introducing a good community-oriented restaurant."
Using fresh North Californian ingredients, "ELKA" serves seafood dishes influenced by French cuisine. The presentation is an ultimate fusion of East and West and the artistic dishes are pleasing to the eyes and tongues of guests.
Designed by Pat Kuleto who, by utilizing the high ceiling and large pillars, the designer has created a gallery-like space with unique lighting appliances made with Japanese paper and metal, wall paintings, etc. from local artists.
＜ELKA＞
Number of guest seats/105
Address/1611 Post Street San Francisco, CA 94115
Phone/415-922-7788

サンフランシスコの「都ホテル」のメインダイニングがこのシーフードレストラン。店名はこのレストランの総料理長 エルカ ギルモア（Elka Gilmore）に由来している。"地元に密着した良いレストランを導入したい"という都ホテル側のバックアップのもとにオープンした。
北カリフォルニア産の新鮮な素材を使用し フランス料理の影響を受けたシーフード料理を提供。東洋と西洋の接点を極めたプレゼンテーションと芸術的な盛り付けでお客の目と舌を楽しませている。
デザインは Pat Kuletoで 高い天井と大きな柱を活かし 和紙やメタルのユニークな照明器具 壁面の絵画など地元のアーティストの作品を利用して ギャラリー風なデザインでまとめている。
〈エルカ〉
客席数/105席
Address/1611 Post Street San Francisco, CA 94115
Phone/415-922-7788

1/ Looking up at the staircase area leading to the 2nd floor lounge; decorated with a glass objet of tropical fish to give a seafood impression.
2/ The dining area viewed from the 2nd floor lounge; the interior layout utilizes the high-ceiled space and large pillars.
3/ The facade.
4/ The window shade imaging a paper sliding screen.

1/2階 ラウンジへの階段廻りをみあげる ガラスの熱帯魚のオブジェが飾られシーフードを印象づけている
2/2階ラウンジからダイニングエリアをみる 高い天井空間と大きな柱を活かした店内構成をしている
3/ファサード
4/障子をイメージした窓のシェード

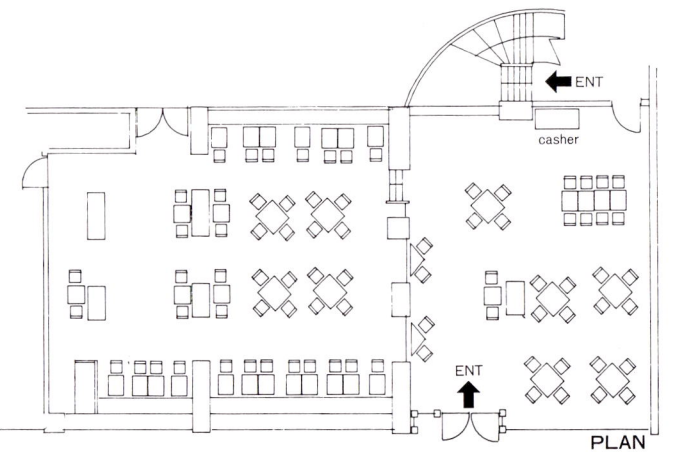

(a)

(b)

(c)

(d)

5/Incorporates elements constituting the "gallery restaurant concept" such as lighting appliances made by using Japanese paper and metal and wall paintings.
6/Overlooking the dining area from the lounge.
7/The chef Elka Gilmore offers fish dishes fusing the East and West.

⑦

5/和紙やメタルを使用した照明器具や壁面の絵画など ギャラリーレストランのコンセプトを取り入れている
6/ラウンジよりダイニングエリアをみおろす
7/料理長の Elka Gilmore は東洋と西洋をマッチさせた 魚料理を提供

●menu
a : TUNA TARTARE ON SUSHI RICE.
b : KAZU MARINATED STURGEON WITH GRILLED RICE AND PRESERVED PLUMS.
c : SAUTEED GROUPER WITH TOMATOES, ARUGULA AND HONEY-ROSEMARY VINAIGRETTE.
d : LEMON MASCARPONE TARTLET.

WATER GRILL
⟨Los Angels⟩

A seafood restaurant opened in downtown Los Angeles by the University Restaurant Group (headquartered in Long Beach). The interior space is composed of the dining area and oyster bar installed against large columns. To create an image of the 1940s as the design concept, paintings by Ann Field, lighting by Pam Morris and other elements are used so that a dignified atmosphere is created.

In this quarter, since a restaurant having an oyster bar is rare, it is gaining popularity with a day-by-day menu whose items are cooked by using more than 40 types of fresh fish ordered from different parts of America. Their motto is "Guests First."

⟨WATER GRILL⟩
Number of guest seats/200 (dining 125, bar 75)
Address/523 West Sixth Street Los Angeles, CA 90014
Phone/213-891-0900

ユニバーシティ レストラン グループ（本社・ロングビーチ）がロサンゼルスのダウンタウンにオープンしたシーフードレストラン。
大きな円柱が立ち並ぶ店内は　ダイニングとオイスターバーで構成され1940年代をイメージしたデザインコンセプトで　壁面のアン フィールド（Ann Field）の描いた壁画　パム モリス（Pam Morris）による照明などが重厚な雰囲気を醸し出している。この周辺にはオイスターバーのあるレストランは珍しく　"ゲスト ファースト（お客様第一）"をモットーにアメリカ各地で水揚げされる40種類以上の新鮮な魚介類の日変わりメニューを提供　人気になっている。
〈ウォーターグリル〉
客席数/200席（ダイニング 125席　バー 75席）
Address/523 West Sixth Street Los Angeles, CA 90014
Phone/213-891-0900

①

②

③

1/ The approach to the reception viewed from the entrance; with wall paintings by Ann Field.
2/ The restaurant viewed from the waiting area.
3/ The facade; covered with glass through which the interior can be looked at.
4/ The bar area; with lighting by Pam Morris.
5/ The restaurant viewed from the bar area.
6/ The oyster bar; appeared for the first time in downtown Los Angeles.

1/エントランスからレセプションへのアプローチをみる　壁画は Ann Field の作品
2/ウェイティングエリアからレストランをみる
3/ファサード　ガラス張りで店内がよくみえる
4/バーエリア　照明は Pam Morris の作品
5/バーエリアからレストランをみる
6/オイスターバー　ロスのダウンタウンでは初めての登場

167

⑦

PLAN

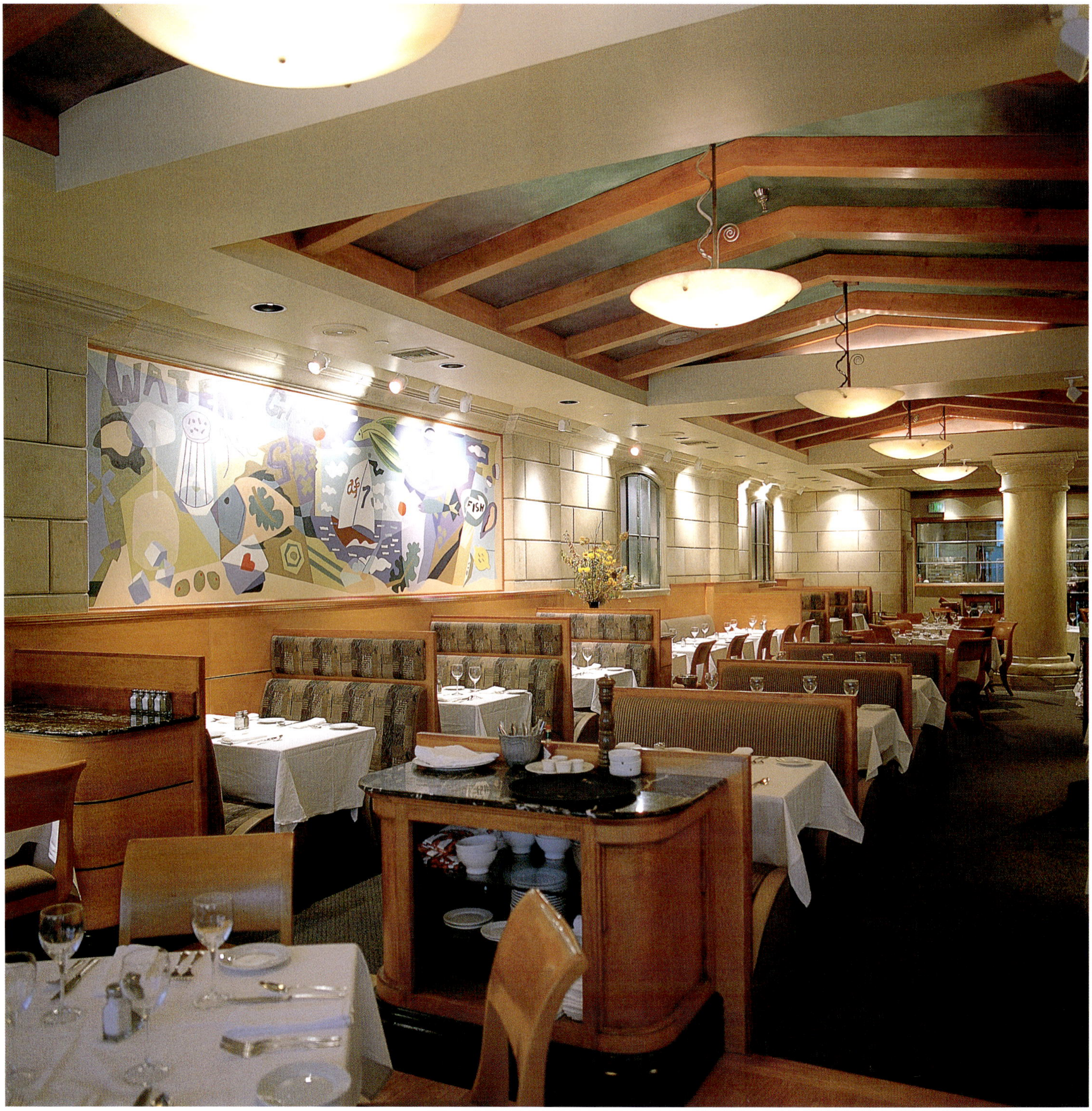

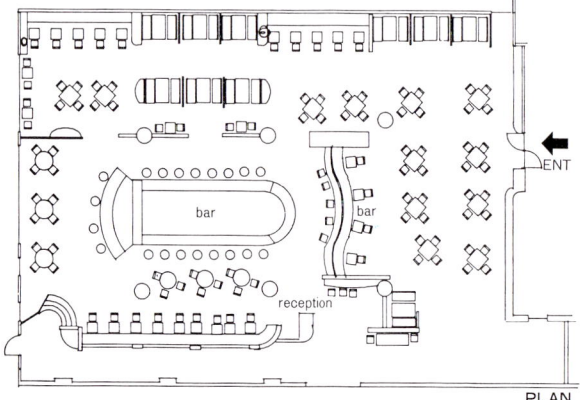

7/The main dining area; creating an image of the 1940s.

7/メインダイニング 1940年代のイメージを醸し出している

●*menu*
a : FRUITS OF THE SEA PLATTER.
b : GRILLED SWORDFISH, ROSEMARY AND GRILLED VEGETABLES.
c : NICOISE SALAD.
d : TROUT FILLETS WITH APPLEWOOD SMOKED BACON.

GRILL
PACIFIC NORTHWEST
ROASTED LINGCOD WITH SAVORY ARTICHOKES AND SHIITAKES 16.75
SAUTEED PETRALE SOLE WITH GOOSEBERRIES 17.50
BROILED HALIBUT, LEMON PEPPER VODKA SAUCE 17.75
STEAMED COLUMBIA RIVER SILVER SALMON 20.25
GRILLED ALASKAN KING SALMON WITH LEMON VERBENA SAUCE 20.25
POACHED ALASKAN KING SALMON, HERB BEURRE BLANC 20.25
HAWAII
GRILLED ALBACORE WITH MAUI ONION CONFIT 17.25
SEARED ONO IN A SPICY LEMONGRASS BROTH 19.00
ROASTED MAHI MAHI WITH TOMATO GINGER CHUTNEY 18.50
SEARED RARE "PEPPERED" AHI WITH PASSION FRUIT BROTH 18.75
GULF OF MEXICO
BLACKENED THRESHER SHARK REMOULADE 15.50
BAKED GROUPER VERA CRUZ 18.25
CALIFORNIA COAST
BARBEQUED YELLOWTAIL WITH TOMATO SALAD
GRILLED SWORDFISH, ROSEMARY AND GRILLED VEGETABLES
SAUTEED SWORDFISH WITH GRAIN MUSTARD SAUCE
SAUTEED GARLIC SPOT PRAWNS WITH ROE
SAUTEED STRIPED BASS WITH COCKLES
CIOPPINO
ATLANTIC COAST
GRILLED SEA SCALLOPS WITH SMOKED TOMATO SAUCE 18.75
TILEFISH PAN ROAST 19.00
LAKES AND STREAMS
TROUT FILLETS WITH APPLE SMOKED BACON
SOUTHERN PAN FRIED CATFISH WITH FRESH HERBS
LOBSTER AND CRAB
LIVE AND FRESH FROM OUR TANKS
STEAMED DUNGENESS CRAB
MAINE LOBSTER (STEAMED OR STUFFED AND BROILED)
BOTH LOBSTERS AND CRAB ARE AVAILABLE STIR FRIED IN A GINGER AND BLACK BEAN SAUCE
MEATS AND POULTRY
GRILLED MARINATED FLANK STEAK WITH MASHED POTATOES
GRILLED FREE RANGE CHICKEN BREAST WITH FRESH HERBES
SAUTEED FILET MIGNON WITH CABERNET SAUVIGNON
GRILLED LOIN LAMB CHOPS WITH HUCKLEBERRY-CASSIS SAUCE
EXECUTIVE CHEF MATTHEW STEIN
SOUS CHEFS ALLYSON THURBER & FERNANDO UBARIO

GRILL

a

b

GRILL

c

GRILL

d

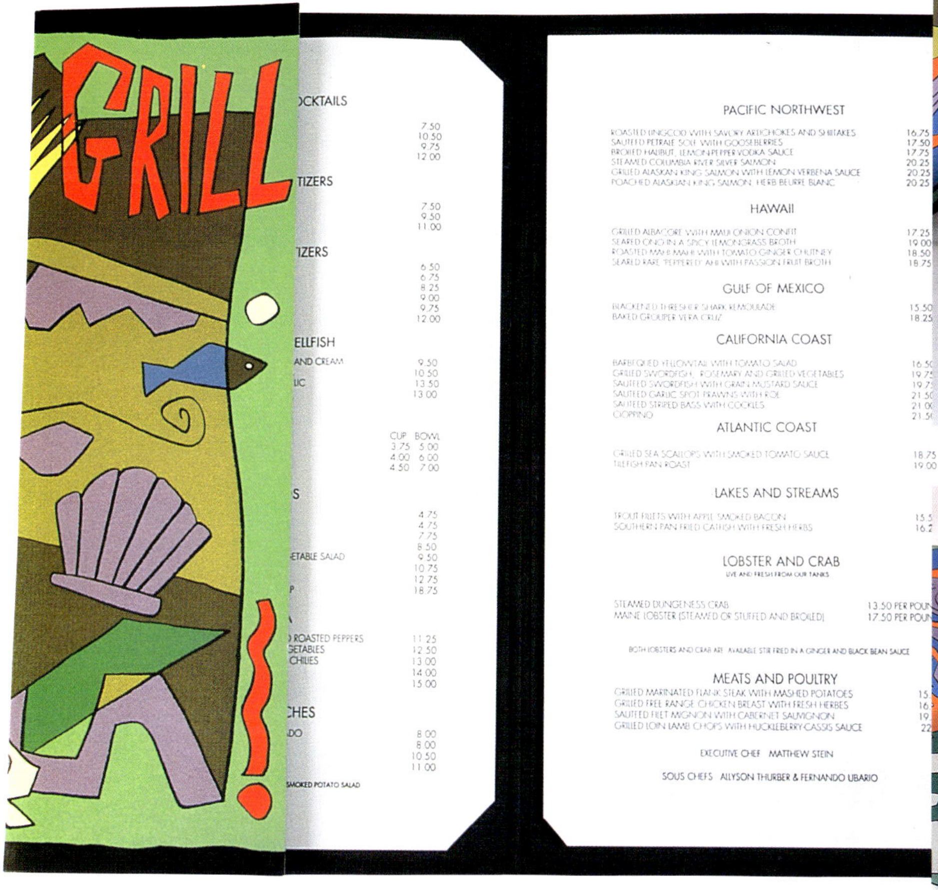

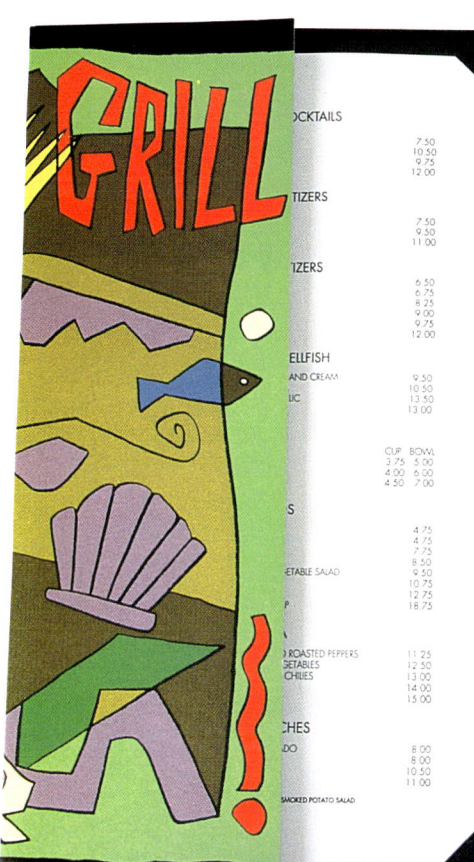

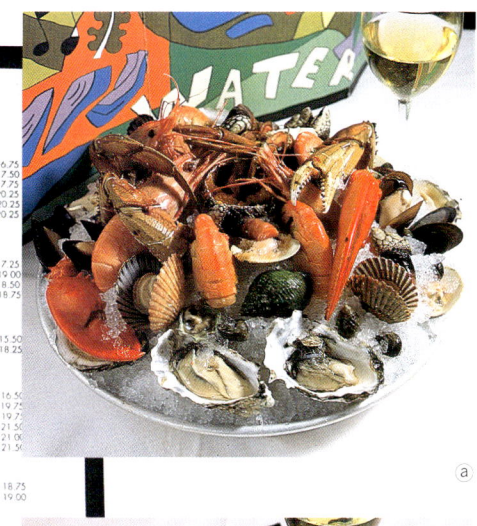

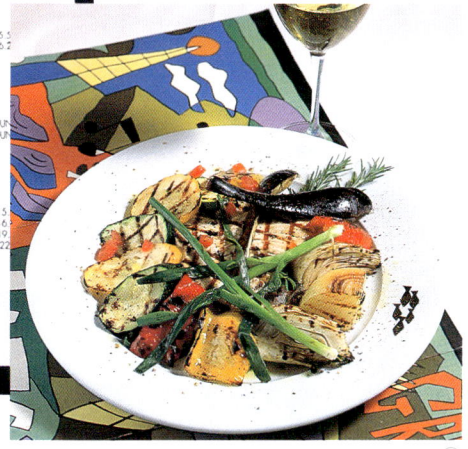

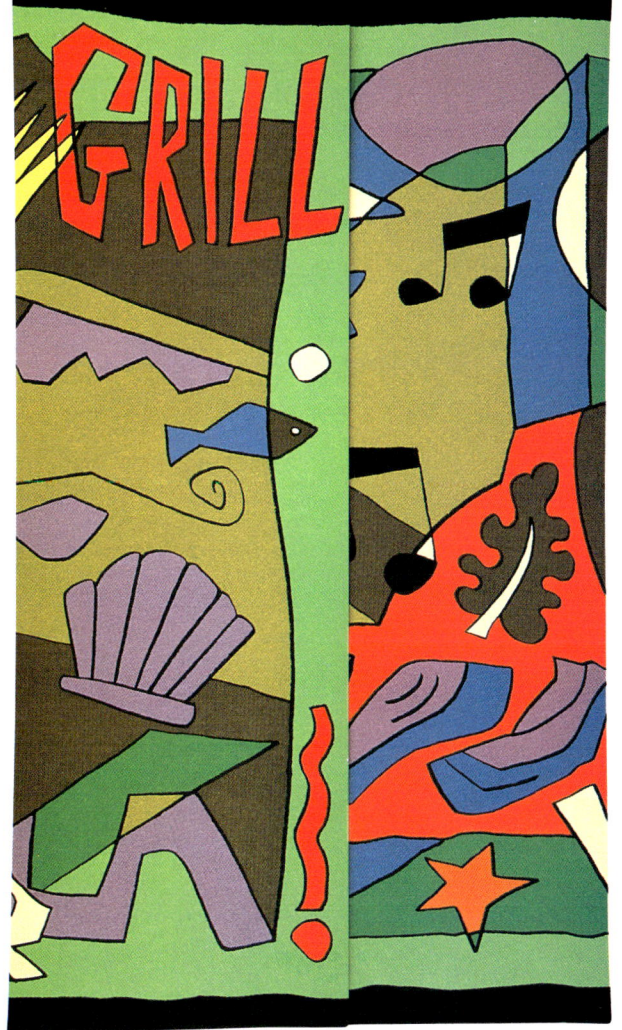

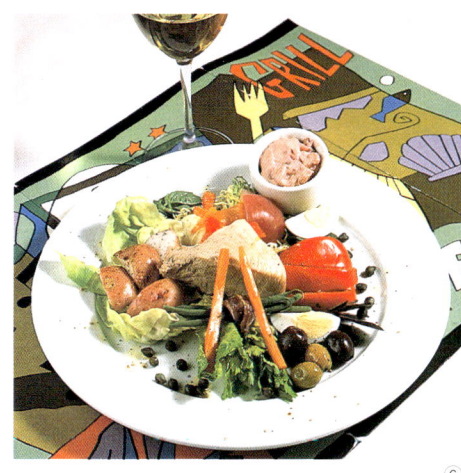

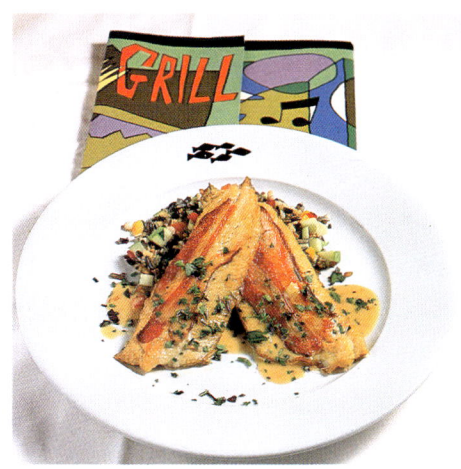

NORTH BEACH BAR & GRILL
⟨Venice⟩

A traditional American grill restaurant on a corner of a condominium, office & shoppng complex near the Venetian sea which is known for Venice Beach. It is popular due to the varied menu items which can be enjoyed casually.
The ideas of the owner Susan Chevalier are permeating every nook and corner of the interior space where a relaxed Californian atmosphere is presented by pursuing themes such as "water," "fish" and "sea." Since very vivid and large pots called California pottery which appeared between the 1920s and 1970s, partitions, a copper-made piece of artistic work expressing a waterfall, etc., which were collected by the owner, are displayed, the interior looks like an art gallery.

<NORTH BEACH BAR & GRILL>
Number of guest seats/150 (dining 100, bar 50)
Address/111 Rose Avenue Venice, CA 90291
Phone/310-399-3900

ベニスビーチで知られるベニス地域の 海に近いコンドミニアムとオフィス＆ショッピングコンプレックス内のコーナーにあるトラディショナルアメリカングリル レストラン。バラエティに富んだメニュー構成と気軽に親しめる料理を提供し人気がある。
店内はオーナーのスーザン シェバリエ（Susan Chevalier）の意志が隅々まで行き届き "水""魚""海"などをテーマにしたカリフォルニアのリラックスした雰囲気を演出している。特にオーナー自身がコレクションした1920〜70年代のカリフォルニア ポタリーと呼ばれる色鮮やかな大きな壺や衝立 銅製の滝を表現した作品などが飾られ アートギャラリーのイメージである。

〈ノースビーチ バー＆グリル〉
客席数/150席（ダイニング 100席 バー 50席）
Address/111 Rose Avenue Venice, CA 90291
Phone/310-399-3900

①

②

③

④

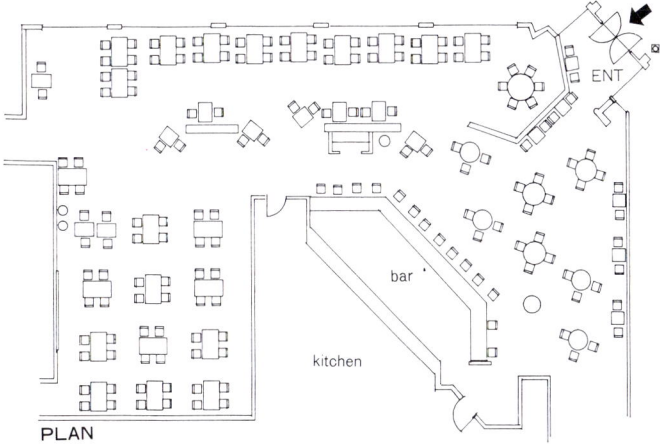
PLAN

1·2/The facade standing out with a huge pierrot; situated on a corner of a condominium, office and shopping complex.
3/The entrance hall; with pots called California pottery which features impressively vivid colors.
4/The bar area.

1·2/大きなピエロが目立つファサード　コンドミニアムとオフィス　ショッピングコンプレックスのコーナーにある
3/エントランスホール　カリフォルニア ポタリーの壺の色が鮮やか
4/バーエリア

172

ⓐ

ⓑ

ⓒ

ⓓ

5/The entrance area of the dining room.
6/The dining room.
7/The wall is decorated with a copper-made piece of artistic work expressing a waterfall and vividly colored pots.

● menu
a : OYSTERS ROCKEFELLER / Fresh Oysters on the half shell baked with Florentine Sauce and Hollandaise.
b : SHELLFISH LINGUINI MARINARA / New Zealand Green Lip Mussels, Clams and Shrimp Sauteed in a Light Marinara.
c : INCREDIBLE GARLIC & ROSEMARY ROASTED CHICKEN / A Half of Chicken Roasted and stuffed with Garlic and Rosemary.
d : NEW YORK 16 oz. STEAK / Prime New York Grilled with Herb Butter.

5/ダイニングルームの入り口廻りをみる
6/ダイニングルームをみる
7/壁面には銅製の滝をイメージした作品や 色鮮やかな壺が飾られている

L'OPERA RISTORANTE
⟨Long Beach⟩

Originally founded by five partners — a management expert, construction company manager, accounting service company manager, restaurant manager and restaurant management professional — it is an Italian restaurant operated by Italatin Inc. which is currently operating 5 restaurants in Southern California, including Giorgio Armani's "Emporio Armani Express" (see page 191).
The restaurant is situated on the 1st floor of a historic building facing Pine Avenue, Long Beach, and secures windows to realize a bright space configuration. The spacious dining area accented with marble columns under the white ceiling, reminds us of the Opera Theater. By installing M-shaped beams on the partition, an etched glass designing the Opera Theater as the shop symbol is inlaid. The display kitchen visible from the dining area is equipped with copper cooking appliances and cooking table creating a gorgeous atmosphere.
Foods served are orthodox Italian cuisine which are voluminous and finely presented by combining vivid colors. Thus, the restaurant is drawing increasingly favorable attention.
<L'OPERA RISTORANTE>
Number of guest seats/342 (dining 173, bar 19, banquet 150)
Address/101 Pine Avenue Long Beach, CA 90802
Phone/310-491-0066

経営のエキスパート　建築会社　経理会社　レストラン経営者そしてレストランマネージメントのプロフェッショナル5人が創業したItalatin Inc.の経営するイタリアンレストラン。現在 南カリフォルニアに5店舗のレストランをマネージメントしている。Giorgio Armaniの「Emporio Armani Express」（本書 191ページ収録）も含まれる。
ロングビーチのパイン アベニュー（Pine Avenue）に面した歴史的なビルの1階のこのレストランは 窓を大きくとり明るい空間構成をしている。白い天井やマーブルの円柱を配した広いダイニングエリアは　オペラ座をイメージさせる。パーティションにM形の梁を設け シンボルマークのオペラ座をデザインしたエッチンググラスがはめ込まれている。ダイニングから見えるディスプレイキッチン内は銅製の調理器具や調理台があり　豪華さを感じさせる。
料理は本格的なイタリア料理で ボリューム 鮮やかな色の組み合わせ プレゼンテーションにいたるまで見事な配慮がなされ話題になっている。
〈ル　オペラ　リストランテ〉
客席数/342席（ダイニング 173席　バー 19席　バンケット 150席）
Address/101 Pine Avenue Long Beach, CA 90802
Phone/310-491-0066

1/ The display kitchen viewed from the dining area through a glass partition.
2/ The marble pillars and bar area viewed from the dining area.
3/ The facade.
4/ The reception area.

1/ダイニングからガラスのパーティション越しにディスプレイキッチンをみる
2/ダイニングからマーブルの柱とバー方向をみる
3/ファサード
4/レセプションをみる

⑤

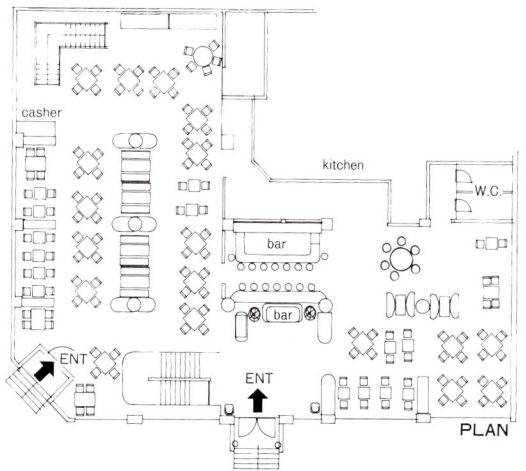

PLAN

⑥

a

b

c

d

5/The wall is decorated with portraits of movie stars.
6/The owner Enzo De Muro (left) and chef Stefano Colaiacomo.

5/壁面には映画スターの似顔絵が飾られている
6/オーナー Enzo De Muro(左) とシェフ Stefano Colaiacomo

●menu
a : ASSAGGINI ALL'ITALIANA /"A Little Bite Italian Style" Four Pastas of Your Choice Served on a Large Platter to Share For Two or More.
b : CARTOCCIO A SORPRESA / Shrimps, Scallops, Tomatoes, Olives Porcini, Mushrooms, Garlic and White Wine, Baked in a Parchment Paper Pauch.
c : TRECCIA D'AGNELLO / Braided Lamb Fillet Grilled, Topped with Butter and Sage. Served with Roasted Potatoes. Polenta and Fresh Vegetables.
d : SOFFICE E LEGGERA /Caramelized Crushed Pineapple Baked over a Light, Tender Sponge Cake, Drizzled with Hot Caramel Sauce and Cream Anglaise.

BIKINI
⟨Santa Monica⟩

A modern ethnic food restaurant which opened in Santa Monica where many trendy restaurants are operating. Occupying the 1st and 2nd floors of a new building occupied by offices, galleries, etc., it introduces a dignified and artistic sense into an open atmosphere with South Western coloring. It is designed by Cheryl Brantner. There are 4 types of dishes plates designed by the owner-chef John Sedlar himself wishing to make guests enjoy tasting his unique modern ethnic cuisine on those plates.
＜BIKINI＞
Number of guest seats/90
Address/1413 Fifth Street Santa Monica, Venice, CA 90401
Phone/213-395-8611   Fax/213-393-9542

トレンディなレストランが多いサンタモニカにオープンしたモダン エスニック料理レストラン。オフィスやギャラリーなどが入居した新しいビルの1・2階の部分を占め サウス ウエスタン調の色や開放的な雰囲気の中に格調とアート感覚を導入している。設計はシェリル ブラントナー(Cheryl Brantner)。オーナー シェフのジョン セドラー(John Sedlar)自身がデザインした盛り付け用の皿が4種類あり 彼独自のモダン エスニック クイジーンのメニューを器でも楽しませながら提供している。
〈ビキニ〉
客席数/90席
Address/1413 Fifth Street Santa Monica, Venice, CA 90401
Phone/213-395-8611   Fax/213-393-9542

①

1/The dining area viewed from the entrance hall; finished by using Southwestern coloring.
2/The open dining area in the 2nd floor stairwell.

1/エントランスホールからダイニングをみる　サウスウエスタン調の色彩で構成している
2/2階吹き抜けの開放的なダイニングエリア

③

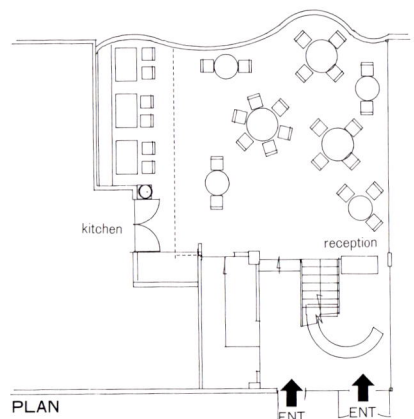

PLAN

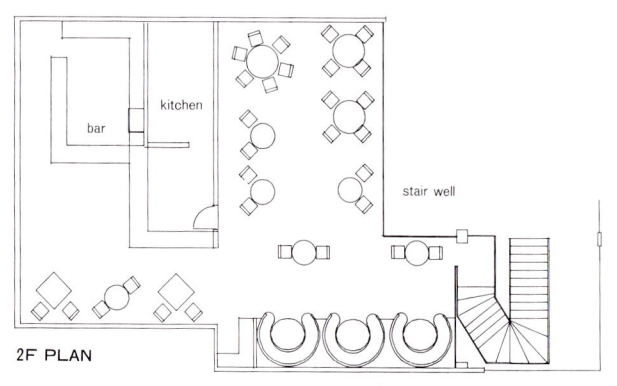

2F PLAN

④

ⓑ

ⓐ

ⓒ

3/The 2nd floor mezzanine seating area; with wall paintings by Muramasa Kudo.
4/The 2nd floor; a colorful booth seating area along the wall.
5/The owner-chef John Sedlar; offers modern ethnic foods in new styles.

⑤

● menu
a : EGG FOO YOUNG DOUBLE HAPPINESS / Scrambled Duck Eggs with Gingered Duck Confit, Sheimija Mushrooms Water Chesnuts, Bamboo Shoots and Scallions, Served in Duck Shells.
b : SUNOMONO SASHIMI SALAD / Nest of Marinated Cucumbers with Spicy Japanese-Style Tuna-Tartare.
c : IVORY TOWER OF WHITE CHOCOLATE MOUSSE.

3/2階 メザニン席 壁面の絵はクドウ ムラマサの作品
4/2階 壁面のカラフルなブース席
5/シェフ オーナー John Sedlar モダン エスニック料理の新スタイルを提供する

181

OPUS RESTAURANT
⟨Santa Monica⟩

A hot spot being talked about as a full-scale, high-class seafood restaurant. It was opened by the owner-chef Eberhard Müller after serving at "Le Bernadin" in New York as executive chef for about 10 years.

Situated on a corner of the new office complex "Water Garden" in Santa Monica, it commands a fine view of an artificial lake. Since several big companies are going to advance into this area, Müller expects that his restaurant will be used by relatively high-level guests from the neighboring offices.

The deep interior space features a warm and elegant atmosphere due to the curvy ceiling lines and glossy Swiss pear wood finish. This has been designed according to the owner's own image of the 1960s Mercedes-Benz. All of the tableware, silverware and glassware are top brand items so that the main dining area gives an impression of one in a high-class hotel.

⟨OPUS RESTAURANT⟩
Number of guest seats/95 (dining 85, bar 10)
Address/2425 West Olympic Blvd. Santa Monica, CA 90404
Phone/310-829-2112

本格的なシーフードの高級店として話題のレストラン。シェフ オーナーのエバーハード ミューラー(Eberhard Müller)がニューヨークの「Le Bernadin」のエグゼクティブ シェフを約10年間務めた後にオープンしたもの。サンタモニカの新しいオフィス コンプレックス 「ウォーターガーデン」の一角に位置し 人工湖の眺めが良く 周辺には大型オフィス数社の進出も予定されおり 比較的高レベルの人たちを客層に見込んでのオープンである。奥行きのある店内は 流れるような天井のラインと光沢のあるスイス ペアウッド(洋梨)を使用したインテリアが暖かさとエレガントな雰囲気を醸し出している。オーナー自身がイメージしたデザインであり 1960年代のメルセデスベンツを想わせるものという。
食器 シルバーウエア グラス類などもトップブランドの製品を使用し 高級ホテルのメインダイニングといった店づくりになっている。
⟨オプス レストラン⟩
客席数/95席(ダイニング 85席 バー 10席)
Address/2425 West Olympic Blvd. Santa Monica, CA 90404
Phone/310-829-2112

1/ The dining area featuring the curvy ceiling design and pear wood finish.
2/ The bar corner.
3/ The appearance of the restaurant and terrace seating area facing the artificial lake of "Water Garden" Complex.
4/ The gently curved full bar counter.

1/流れるような天井のデザインとペアウッド材を使用したダイニング
2/バーコーナーをみる
3/「ウォーターガーデン」コンプレックスの人工湖に面したレストランの外観とテラス席をみる
4/柔らかいカーブを持たせたフルバーのカウンター

183

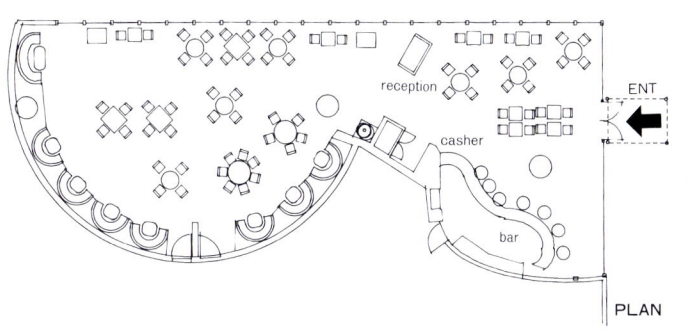

● menu
a : *MAINE LOBSTER WITH TOMATOED LOBSTER BROTH.*
b : *OPUS MILLE FEUILLE.*

5/The dining room imaging a yacht cabin.
6/The composed dining room by the wall.
7/The owner-chef Eberhard Müller (right) and executive chef Ian Winslade.

5/ヨットのキャビンをイメージしたダイニングルーム
6/壁面の落ち着きのあるブース席
7/オーナー シェフ Eberhard Müller(右)とエグゼクティブシェフ Ian Winslade

PINOT BISTRO
⟨Studio City⟩

The owner-chef Joachim Splichal has been the talk of the town, as he was named the "Best California Chef" for 1991 by the James Beard Society, and in 1992 this restaurant was ranked No. 1 in Southern California in the Zagat Restaurant Guide. By purchasing "La Serre" which continued to run for 18 years, he has renovated it into this restaurant.

It was designed by Cheryl Brantner who is active mainly in Los Angeles. In preparation for the opening, he traveled across Europe together with the owner to see various pieces of furniture and interior, and absorbed the atmosphere of traditional French bistros into their own shop making. Beige walls, a dark brown wooden door, a counter, a large wine cabinet, letters drawn on the mirror, floor tiles which look like waving black & white, white tablecloth, etc. – all these are arranged in an orthodox bistro style.

⟨PINOT BISTRO⟩
Number of guest seats/170 (dining 160, bar 10)
Address/12969 Ventura Boulevard Studio City, CA 91604
Phone/818-990-0500

オーナー シェフの Joachim Splichal は ジェームス ビアード協会 (James Beard Society)の 1991年 "ベスト カリフォルニア シェフ" 1992年には Zagatレストランガイドで 南カリフォルニアでナンバーワンにランクされた 話題のシェフ。18年間続いたレストラン「ラ セール(La Serre)」を買収しリニューアル オープンしたもの。
デザインはロサンゼルスを中心に活躍する Cheryl Brantner。
オープンするにあたってはオーナーとともにヨーロッパを巡り 家具やインテリアを見ると同時に 伝統的なフランスのビストロの雰囲気も吸収し 店づくりにとり入れている。ベージュの壁 濃いブラウンの木製のドアやカウンター 大きなワインキャビネット ミラーの上に描かれた文字 白と黒が波打つ感じのフロアタイル 白いテーブルクロスなど本格的なビストロのスタイルである。

⟨ピノ ビストロ⟩
客席数/170席(ダイニング 160席 バー 10席)
Address/12969 Ventura Boulevard Studio City, CA 91604
Phone/818-990-0500

①

1/ The dining area viewed from the reception area.
2/ The dining room in a French provincial style.
3/ The facade/entrance area.
4/ A large wine cabinet on the entrance hall.

1/レセプションよりダイニングをみる
2/フランスの田舎家風のダイニングルーム
3/ファサード　エントランス廻りをみる
4/エントランスホールの大きなワインキャビネット

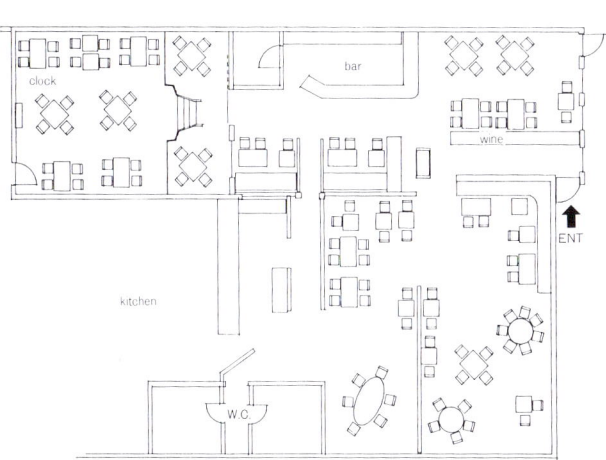

5/The dining area designed to give a traditional French bistro image.
6/The bar area.
7/Unique wall panels and lighting design.

5/伝統的なフランスのビストロの雰囲気を持たせたダイニング
6/バーエリアをみる
7/ユニークな壁面のパネルと照明のデザイン

8/The owner-chef Joachim Splichal.

8/シェフ オーナー　Joachim Splichal

● menu
a : Sauted Scallops with Eggplant Puree and Valley Pistou source.
b : Napoleon of Halbut, Zucchini, Tomatoes and Basil.
c : Oxtail Ragout and Parsley Gnocchi.
d : Crunchy Chocolate Cake with Mocha Sauce.

EMPORIO ARMANI EXPRESS
⟨Costa Mesa⟩

Giorgio Armani, a representative Italian fashion designer, realized his first attempt at introducing his restaurant operations into the U.S.A. This restaurant was juxtaposed to his boutique in the shopping center, "South Coast Plaza," in Costa Mesa.
Against a casual setting, the interior heavily uses wood, accented with blue cushions in contrast to the blond color as the basic tone. Blue Armani marks are designed on all of the white napkins, menus, plates, uniforms, etc.
Centering around Italian foods, the menu items are mainly composed with emphasis on simple and fresh features.
It is managed by GA Eatery Inc., an affiliate of the Armani group, and operated by Italatin Inc.
<EMPORIO ARMANI EXPRESS>
Number of guest seats/80
Address/South Coast Plaza 3333 Bristol Street Costa Mesa, CA 92626
Phone/714-754-0300

イタリアを代表するファッションデザイナー Giorgio Armani がアメリカにはじめてレストラン部門の進出をした。コスタメサのショッピングセンター サウス コースト プラザ内の彼のブティックに併設したもの。カジュアルなセッティングの中に 木を多用し ブロンドカラーを基調に ブルーのクッションをアクセントにしている。ナプキン メニュー 料理皿 ユニフォームなどすべて白地で ブルーのアルマーニのマークがデザインされている。
料理はイタリア料理を中心にした構成で シンプルでフレッシュさを強調している。経営は傘下の GA Eatery Inc.で 運営は Italatin Inc.。
⟨エンポリオ アルマーニ エクスプレス⟩
客席数/80席
Address/South Coast Plaza　3333 Bristol Street Costa Mesa, CA 92626
Phone/714-754-0300

1/The dining area and counter seating space.　　　1/ダイニングとカウンター席方向をみる

2/The gently curved counter seating area.
3/The wine bar facing the shopping center; the right-hand part of the floor, which is higher than the rest, continues to Armani's boutique.
4/An antipasto display table placed in the center of the dining room.

2/緩やかなカーブを持たせたカウンター席
3/ショッピングセンターに面したワインバーをみる
　右側はフロアアップしてアルマーニのブティックに続いている
4/ダイニングルーム中央に置かれたアンティパストのディスプレイテーブル

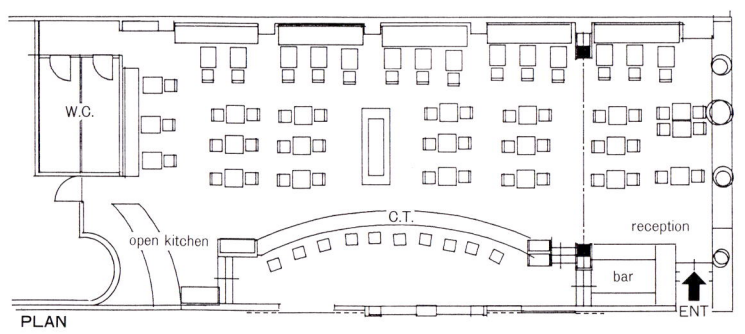

PLAN

● menu
a : CARPACCIO ALLA ROMANA / Thin slices of raw beef topped with parmigiano cheese and arugula.
b : DI CARCIOFI / Artichokes, topped with finely sliced parmesan cheese.
c : AL SALMONE / Topped with smoked salmon and mozzarela.

L'ESCOFFIER
⟨Beverly Hills⟩

"L'ESCOFFIER" is a high-class French restaurant on the top floor of the Beverly Hilton Hotel in Beverly Hills.
Since its opening in 1955 it had been operated by the former owner and in 1985 Merv Griffin became the owner and the interior was redecorated into a bright and elegant one from the dignified atmosphere in the 1950s~1960s.
With a dance floor and lounge, the interior space is generally finished in an ivory tone; from large windows guests can command a view of Bevery Hills and Hollywood scenery which is also reflected in the mirrors on the wall of the booth seating area, thus creating an open atmosphere.
Under the chef Michael Blanchet who was recently brought in, the restaurant offers a menu harmoniously composed of traditional French and Californian foods.
<L'ESCOFFIER>
Address/Beverly Hilton Hotel
　　　　9876 Wilshire Blvd. Beverly Hills, CA
Phone/310-274-7777

ビバリーヒルズのビバリー ヒルトンホテル（Beverly Hilton Hotel）の最上階の高級フランス料理レストラン。1955年に開店のこのレストランは1985年にオーナーが Merv Griffin に変わり レストランも '50～60の重厚な雰囲気から 明るいエレガントなデザインにリニューアルされた。ダンスフロアとラウンジを設けた店内は全体にアイボリーを基調にまとめられ 大きくとった窓からはビバリーヒルズやハリウッドの風景が眺められ それがブース席の壁面に貼られたミラーにも写り込み 開放的な雰囲気である。シェフに新しくMichel Blanchet を迎え 伝統的なフランス料理とカリフォルニア料理を交差させたメニューを提供している。
〈エスコフィエ〉
Address/Beverly Hilton Hotel
　　　　9876 Wilshire Blvd. Beverly Hills, CA
Phone/310-274-7777

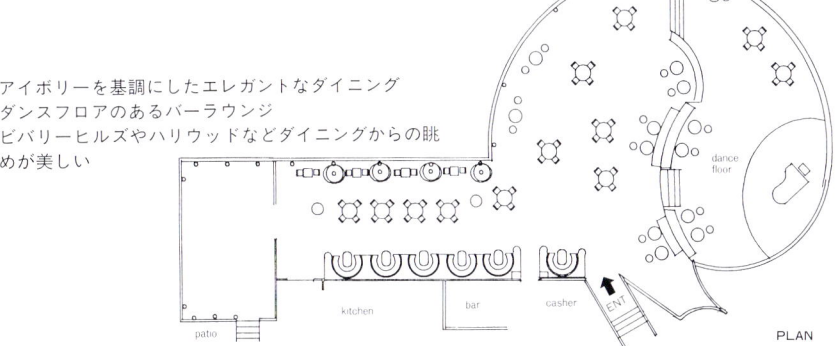

1/The elegant dining room finished by using ivory as the basic tone.
2/The bar lounge having a dance floor.
3/From the dining room guests can command a wonderful view of Beverly Hills and Hollywood.

1/アイボリーを基調にしたエレガントなダイニング
2/ダンスフロアのあるバーラウンジ
3/ビバリーヒルズやハリウッドなどダイニングからの眺めが美しい

PLAN

ⓐ

ⓑ

④

4/The chef Michel Blanchet (right) and manager Fernand Poitras.

4/シェフ Michel Blanchet（右）とマネジャー Fernand Poitras

ⓒ

ⓓ

●menu
a : Broiled Tuna Tournedos, Oriental Spices.
b : Duck Liver Salad with Fresh Artichoke and Truffles.
c : Roasted Duck Magret, Apple and Ginger Flan, Sweet Onions and Chardonnay Sauce.
d : Raspberry Mille Feuilles, Caramel Sauce.

PICNIC
⟨Los Angeles⟩

This restaurant faces Pico Blvd. which is close to Century City. It is a so-called American style bistro where foods can be enjoyed "light-heartedly, casually and cheaply." The owner-chef is Claude Segal who was once the second chef of "Ma Maison."
With landscapes painted on the wall, the interior is designed to give a terrace-like image and uses mirrors to create a spacious impression. Due to the casual and homely atmosphere, "PICNIC" looks like a restaurant in the suburbs of France in the 1970s. It is crowded with a variety of guests such as neighborhood inhabitants, those engaged in the film or music business in Hollywood and related businessmen.
⟨PICNIC⟩
Address/8771 Pico Blvd. Los Angeles, CA
Phone/310-723-1166

センチュリーシティに近い ピコ大通り（Pico Blvd.）に面したレストラン。料理を"気軽に 気どりなく 安価に"楽しめる いわゆるアメリカンビストロと呼ばれるスタイルで オーナー シェフはクロード シーガル（Claude Segal）。彼は「Ma Maison」の2代目のシェフだった人。
壁面には風景画が描かれ テラスをイメージさせるインテリアでミラーを使用して広さを感じさせる演出をしている。気どりのない家庭的な雰囲気は 1970年代のフランス郊外のレストランといった感じで 近隣の住民はじめ ハリウッドの映画やミュージック関係者 ビジネス客など巾広い客層で賑っている。
⟨ピクニック⟩
Address/8771 Pico Blvd. Los Angeles, CA
Phone/310-273-1166

1・2/The dining room; designed like a terrace.
3/The facade.

1・2/ダイニングルーム テラスを演出している
3/ファサード

④

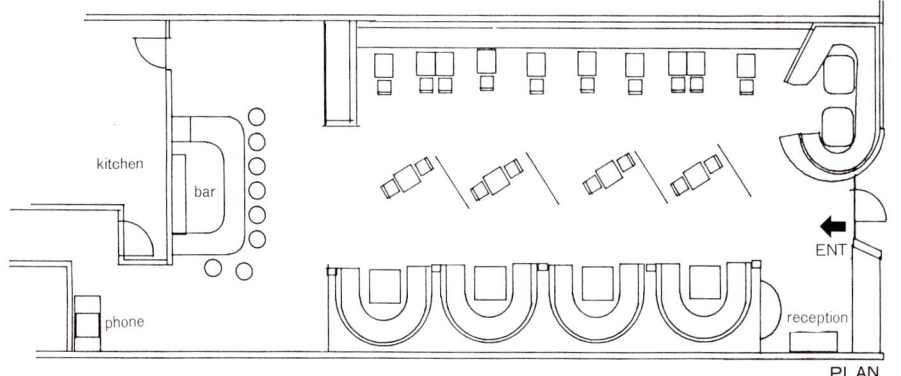

PLAN

⑤

(a)

(b)

(c)

(d)

4/The back of the bench seating area is covered with mirrors in which the wall paintings are reflected so that the interior space looks expansive.
5/The bar corner; appears to have a large depth due to a wine rack which also uses a mirror.
6/The owner-chef Claude Segal.

4/ベンチ席の後ろにはミラーが貼られ 壁画が映りこみ 広がりを感じさせる
5/バーコーナー ワインラックにもミラーがはめ込まれ 奥行きを感じさせる
6/オーナー シェフ Claude Segal

⑥

● menu
a : Baked Layers of Filo Dough with Asparagus, Goat Cheese & Tomato.
b : Steak of Whitefish in Coarse Black Peppers & Shredded Leeks, Served with Petite Syrah Reduction.
c : Crispy Sauted Sweetbreads with Zuccini Blossom & Wild Mushrooms, Served with a Small Reduction of Cabernet.
d : Flourless Chocolate Cake with Tree Sorbets.

TATOU
⟨Beverly Hills⟩

This restaurant reminds us of "Coconut Grove," a night club which once existed in Hollywood in the 1940s. The high ceiling is covered over with drapes, and a large antique chandelier is suspended from the center of the draped surface. 10 palm trees whose trunks are wound round with fiber, are 13 feet high, and whose leaves are made of copper and nuts serve as lighting appliances. Golden leaves are pictured on the walls of the booth seating area, and coconut-shaped lamps are placed on the tables.

The mirrors and paintings decorating the wall are a private collection of the actor Tony Curtis. On the stage which stands against a piece of deep magenta cloth, blues or POP music is performed. Mark Fleischman serves as manager and creator. The design was undertaken by HaVerson Rockwell Architects in New York and Cannon Bullock, a design company in Los Angeles.

The menu features creative items incorporating provincial ingredients. The chef is Desi Szonntagh.

⟨TATOU⟩
Number of guest seats/210 (dining 140, bistro 60, bar 10)
Address/233 N. Beverly Drive Beverly Hills, CA 90210
Phone/310-274-9965

1940年代 ハリウッドにあったナイトクラブ「ココナッツ グローブ」をイメージさせるレストラン。高い天井にドレイプを張り巡らせ その中央にはアンティークの大きなシャンデリアがある。樹幹に繊維を巻いた10本のパームツリーは13フィートの高さで 葉は銅製 果実は照明になっている。ブース席の壁面には金色の葉がデザインされ テーブルの上には椰子の形のランプが置かれている。

壁面に飾られた鏡や絵画は 俳優のトニー カーチス(Tony Curtis)のプライベイト コレクション。深いマゼンタ色の布を背景にしたステージではブルースやポップミュージックが演奏される。経営兼クリーエイターは Mark Fleischman。デザインはニューヨークの Haverson Rockwell Architects と ロサンゼスのデザイン会社 Cannon Bullock。

プロヴァンス地方の料理を反映させたクリエイティブなメニュー構成でシェフは Desi Szonntagh。

⟨タトー⟩
客席数/210席(ダイニング 140席 ビストロ 60席 バー 10席)
Address/233 N. Beverly Drive Beverly Hills, CA 90210
Phone/310-274-9955

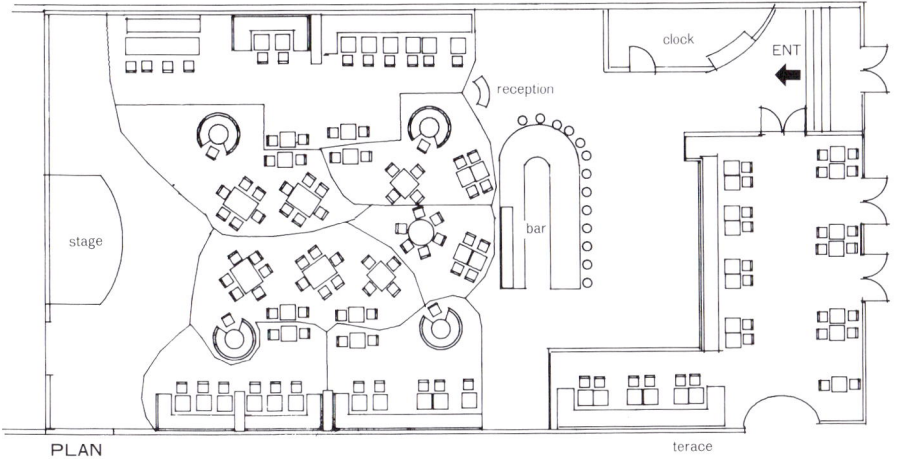

PLAN

1/ The dining room; with palm tree nuts serving as lighting appliances.
2/ The facade/entrance area.
3/ The service counter with a wine cabinet; continuous with the bar behind the counter.
4/ The interior designed in an image of night club "Coconut Grove" which existed in Hollywood in the 1940s.

1/ダイニングのパームツリーの実が照明になっている
2/ファサード　エントランス廻りをみる
3/ワインキャビネットのあるサービスカウンター　裏側のバーとつながっている
4/1940年代のハリウッドのナイトクラブ「ココナッツグローブ」をイメージさせるインテリア

(a)

(b)

(c)

● menu
a : Devilled Crab Cake with Cilantro Mayonnaise and Corn Relish.
Grilled Tuna with Sasame Ginger Dressing.
House Smoked Salmon with Dill Pancakes and Creme Fraiche.
b : Shrimp and Lobster with Raspberry Vinaigrette and Creme Fraiche.
c : Poached Salmon with Avocado and Three Caviars.

5/The bar counter.

5/バーカウンターをみる

(5)

LUMA
⟨Santa Monica⟩

Montana Av., Santa Monica, is very popular as a fashionable street crowded with unique boutiques and restaurants. This restaurant, whose main shop is in New York, has advanced onto this avenue, aimed at inviting sophisticated people to experience the world of new foods by offering a menu mainly composed of healthy vegetables and seafoods. For this purpose, the chef Robert Smith and manager/joint operator Eric Stapleton were invited from the main shop to introduce the common concept.

The interior uses a combination of wood, glass and iron, and also uses a skylight effectively so that the interior space is very bright. The restaurant was designed by Cheryl Brantner who uses moderate colors on the wall, floor, chair cushions, etc., and accentuates naturalness by decorating with seasonal flowers. Monotonous abstract paintings on the wall, simple pieces of art, white tablecloth — all these are conducive to creating a simple but elegantly composed atmosphere.

<LUMA>
Number of guest seats/101 (dining 95, bar 6)
Address/1323 Montana Av. Santa Monica, CA
Phone/310-451-0900

サンタモニカのモンタナ アベニュー(Montana Av.)は ユニークなブティックやレストランが集まるファッショナブルな通りとして人気が高い。ニューヨークに本店を持つこのレストランが ここに進出したのもソフィスティケートされた人々を対象に健康的なイメージの野菜やシーフードを中心としたメニュー構成で 新しい料理の世界を体験してもらおうというねらいである。そのために本店からシェフ Robert Smith やマネジャーで共同経営者 Eric Stapleton を迎え 共通のコンセプトを導入している。店内は木とガラスと鉄のコンビネーションにスカイライトを効果的に使用し明るい。デザインはCheryl Brantnerで 壁や床 椅子のクッションなどの色をおさえ 自然さを強調 四季折々の花を飾り ポイントにしている。壁面のモノトーンのアブストラクトの絵画や素朴な感じのアート作品 白いテーブルクロスなどシンプルではあるがエレガントな落ち着きを醸し出している。

⟨ルマ⟩
客席数/101席(ダイニング 95席 バー 6席)
Address/1323 Montana Av. Santa Monica, CA
Phone/310-451-0900

1/The reception area viewed from the bar area.　　　1/バーエリアからレセプション方向をみる

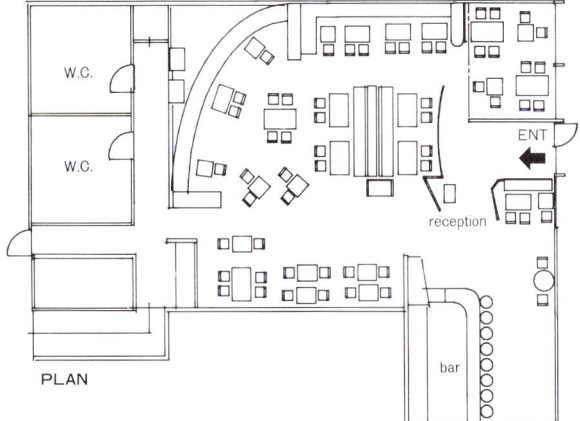

2/The sophisticated and elegant dining room; bright due to a skylight.
3/The bar corner.
4/The facade.

2/ソフィスティケイトされエレガントなダイニング 天窓があり明るい
3/バーコーナーをみる
4/ファサード

⑤

⑥

⑦

5/ The entrance area viewed from an inner part of the dining room.
6/ The entrance hall; with a glass partition and an opening dining area.
7/ A toilet.
8/ The chef Robert Smith (left) and manager/Joint operator Eric Stapleton.

5/ダイニングルーム奥からエントランス方向をみる
6/エントランスホール ガラスのパーティションと開放的なダイニングをみる
7/洗面室をみる
8/シェフRobert Smith(左)とマネジャーで共同経営者のEric Stapleton

(a)

(b)

(c)

(d)

(e)

● menu
a : GRILLED PORTOBELLO MUSHROOMS / with charred endive and radicchio.
b : ROASTED AND GRILLED VEGETABLE PLATE / with mixed grains and roasted vegetable jus.
c : SEARED SALMON WITH TUSCAN PEAS ANT SALAD + BALSAMIC GLAZE.
d : CHOCOLATE DEVASTATION CAKE WITH RASPBERRY COULIS.

207

POST
⟨Sherman Oaks⟩

In recent years, an increasing number of restaurants have come to Sherman Oaks which is situated in the northwestern side of downtown Los Angeles.
"POST" is an Italian restaurant being operated by Piero Selvaggio. By accurately grasping the needs of the times, he has simplified foods and limited the menu to cheaper, but elegant and imaginative items. The chef is Luciano Pellegrini.
The interior is designed by incorporating an artistic sense so that it has a luxurious atmosphere suitable for adults. The design was undertaken by Osvaldo Maiozzi, architect, and Robert W. Burton, designer.
<POST>
Number of guest seats/125
Address/14928 Ventura Blvd. Sherman Oaks, CA 91403
Phone/818-784-4400

ロサンゼルスのダウンタウンの北西に位置するシャーマンオークスはこの数年レストランの出店が著しい地域である。
この店は ピエロ セルヴァジオ（Piero Selvaggio）が経営するイタリア料理レストラン。時代のニーズを的確につかみ 料理のシンプル化と低価格路線で メニューアイテムをしぼり エレガントでイマジネイティブな料理を提供している。シェフはルチアノ ペレグニ（Luciano Pellegrini）。店内はアート感覚を取り入れた店づくりで ラグジュアリィな感じは大人のレストランといえる。デザインは建築家のオズワルド マイオッツィ（Osvaldo Maiozzi）と デザイナーのロバート バートン（Robert W. Burton）。
〈ポスト〉
客席数/125席
Address/14928 Ventura Blvd. Sherman Oaks CA 91403
Phone/818-784-4400

1/The dining area with bench seats installed along the approach from the bar area to the main dining area.
2/The bar corner.
3/A cloth shade; designed as an objet.
4/The main dining area; with pieces of artistic work displayed on the wall.
5/The facade.

1/バーエリアからメインダイニングへのアプローチに設けられたベンチシートのあるダイニング
2/バーコーナーをみる
3/布製のシェイド　デザイン化されている
4/メインダイニング　壁面にはアート作品がディスプレイされている
5/ファサード

⑥

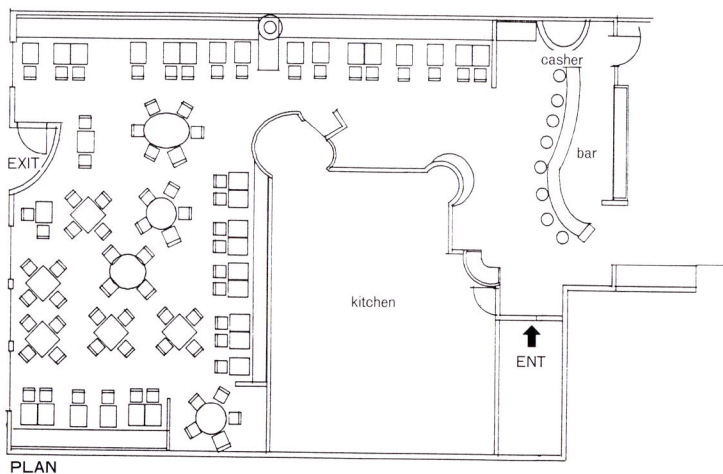

PLAN

⑦

ⓐ

ⓑ

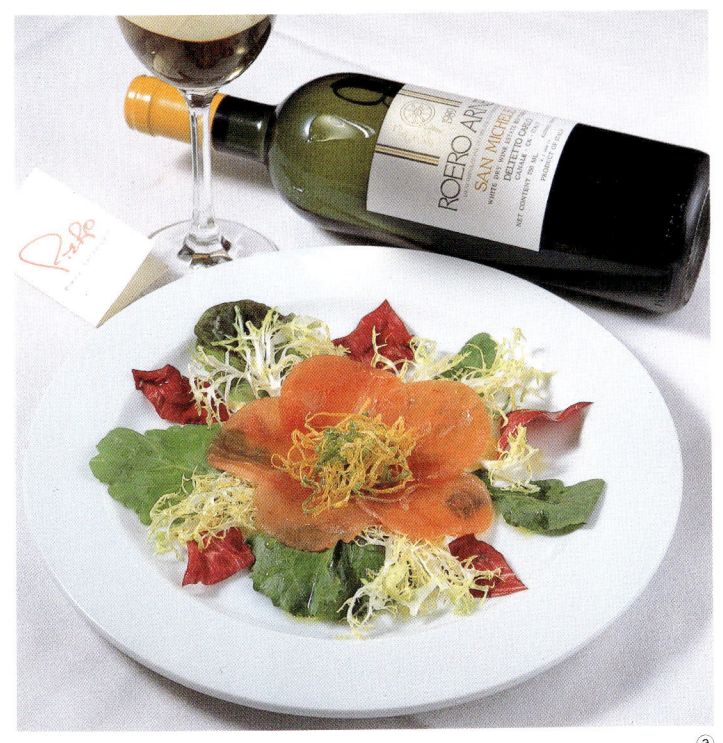

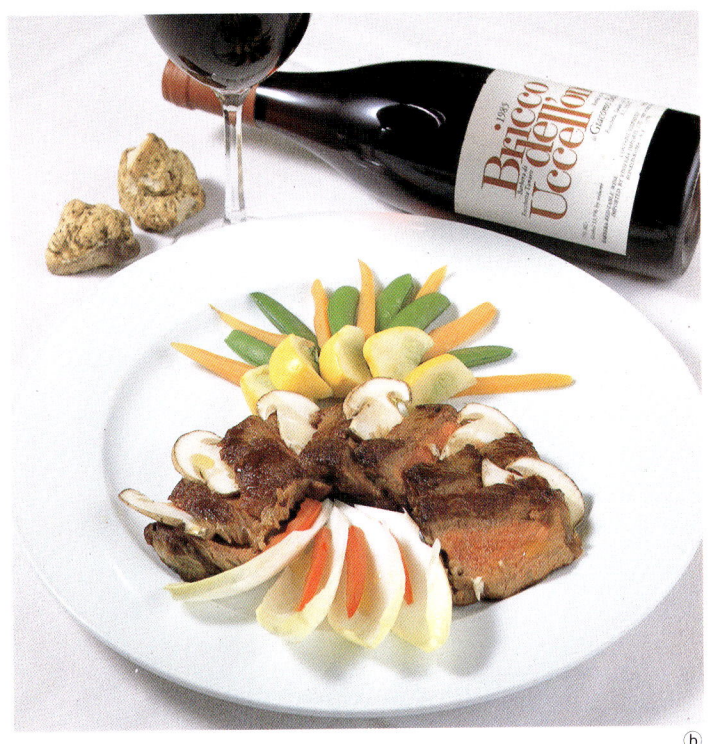

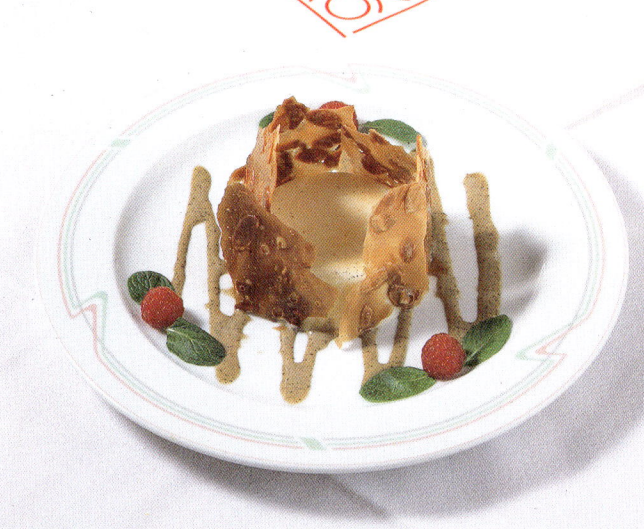

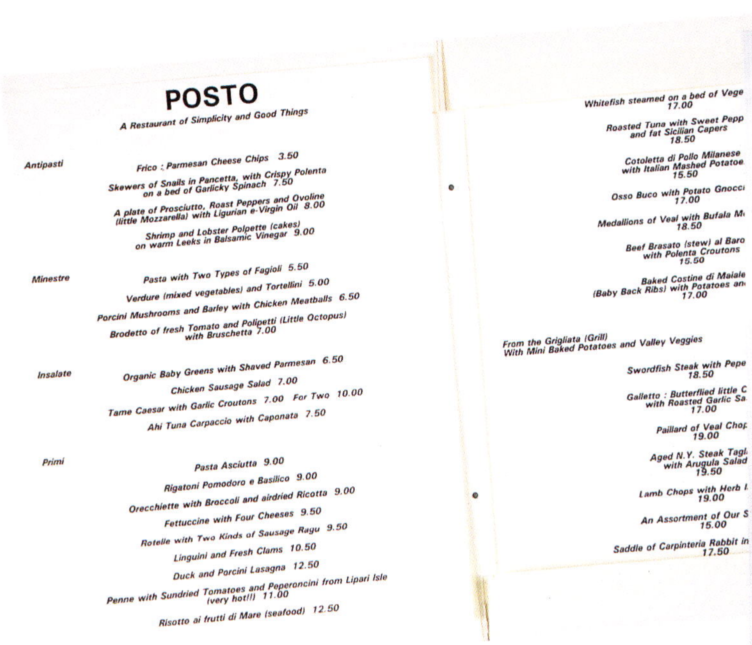

POSTO

A Restaurant of Simplicity and Good Things

Antipasti

Frico : Parmesan Cheese Chips 3.50

Skewers of Snails in Pancetta, with Crispy Polenta on a bed of Garlicky Spinach 7.50

A plate of Prosciutto, Roast Peppers and Ovoline (little Mozzarella) with Ligurian e-Virgin Oil 8.00

Shrimp and Lobster Polpette (cakes) on warm Leeks in Balsamic Vinegar 9.00

Minestre

Pasta with Two Types of Fagioli 5.50

Verdure (mixed vegetables) and Tortellini 5.00

Porcini Mushrooms and Barley with Chicken Meatballs 6.50

Brodetto of fresh Tomato and Polipetti (Little Octopus) with Bruschetta 7.00

Insalate

Organic Baby Greens with Shaved Parmesan 6.50

Chicken Sausage Salad 7.00

Tame Caesar with Garlic Croutons 7.00 For Two 10.00

Ahi Tuna Carpaccio with Caponata 7.50

Primi

Pasta Asciutta 9.00

Rigatoni Pomodoro e Basilico 9.00

Orecchiette with Broccoli and airdried Ricotta 9.00

Fettuccine with Four Cheeses 9.50

Rotelle with Two Kinds of Sausage Ragu 9.50

Linguini and Fresh Clams 10.50

Duck and Porcini Lasagna 12.50

Penne with Sundried Tomatoes and Peperoncini from Lipari Isle (very hot!!) 11.00

Risotto ai frutti di Mare (seafood) 12.50

Whitefish steamed on a bed of Vege
17.00

Roasted Tuna with Sweet Pepp
and fat Sicilian Capers
18.50

Cotoletta di Pollo Milanese
with Italian Mashed Potatoe
15.50

Osso Buco with Potato Gnocc
17.00

Medallions of Veal with Bufala M
18.50

Beef Brasato (stew) al Baro
with Polenta Croutons
15.50

Baked Costine di Maiale
(Baby Back Ribs) with Potatoes an
17.00

From the Grigliata (Grill)
With Mini Baked Potatoes and Valley Veggies

Swordfish Steak with Pepe
18.50

Galletto : Butterflied little C
with Roasted Garlic Sa
17.00

Paillard of Veal Chop
19.00

Aged N.Y. Steak Tagl
with Arugula Salad
19.50

Lamb Chops with Herb
19.00

An Assortment of Our S
15.00

Saddle of Carpinteria Rabbit in
17.50

ⓒ

6/The dining room; designed artistically.
7/The corner with a wine cellar; also used as a private room.
8/The owner Piero Selvaggio (left) and chef Luciano Pellegrini.

6/アーティスティックにデザインされたダイニングルーム
7/ワインセラーのあるコーナー　プライベートルームとしても使用される
8/オーナー Piero Selvaggio（左）とシェフ Luciano Pellegrini

⑧

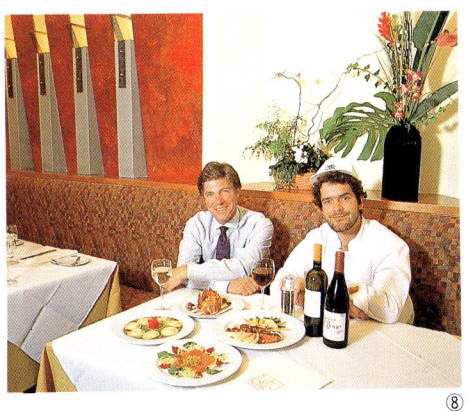

●menu
a : TUNA CARPACCIO WITH MIXED GREENS MARINATED WITH CITRUS ZEST & EX. VERGIN OLIVE OIL.
b : AGED NEW YORK STEAK TAGLIATA WITH PORCINI MUSHROOMS.
c : PANNA COTTA W/CARAMELIZED ALMONDS ESPRESSO CREME ANGLAIS.

MODELLA RISTORANTE
⟨San Francisco⟩

This Italian restaurant is situated in an area called North Beach in the financial street of San Francisco. This area is adjacent to China Town and Italian Street.

The interior features a contemporary design and, with the intense terra-cotta color as the basic tone, moderate gold stripes and sensual human prints are placed on the wall and pillars, thus creating a sophisticated atmosphere. The design was undertaken by Michael Brennan. Having about 300 seats, this restaurant is very large and composed of the main dining area, private dining "Le Club Room" and bar area. Also, by installing booth seats and small rooms, or accenting the interior with lighting and coloring to prevent guests from having a too spacious impression, a composed atmosphere is presented.

Chef Lorretta Rampone, who is also one of the owners, studied at a cooking school in Tuscany, Italy, and worked under Signora Lorenza Demedici, an authority on Italian cuisine. He is counted as one of the star chefs in San Francisco.

⟨MODELLA RISTORANTE⟩
Number of guest seats/300 (dining 120, private room 120, bar 60)
Address/7 Spring Street San Francisco, CA 94108
Phone/415-362-1990

サンフランシスコの金融街の中　チャイナタウンとイタリアン街に隣接する　いわゆるノースビーチ(North Beach)と呼ばれる地域にあるイタリア料理レストラン。

店内はコンテンポラリィな造りで　強烈なテラコッタの色を基調に　おさえめの金色のストライプや官能的な人物のプリントを壁面や柱に配しソフィスティケイトされた雰囲気である。デザインはマイケル ブレナン(Michael Brennan)。メインダイニング　プライベートダイニングの"Le Club Room"とバーエリアで構成される約300席の大きなレストランであるが　ブース席や小部屋を設けたり　照明やカラーリングで変化をつけることで　広さを感じさせない落ち着いた雰囲気の演出をしている。

　オーナーの一人でシェフのロレッタ ランポーネ(Loretta Rampone)は　イタリアのタスカニイ(Tuscany)地方の料理学校に学び　イタリア料理のオーソリティ シグノラ ロレンザ デメディチ(Signora Lorenza Demedici)の下で働いた経験を持つ人で　サンフランシスコのスターシェフに数えられている。

⟨モデラ リストランテ⟩
客席数/300席(ダイニング 120席　個室 120席　バー 60席)
Address/7 Spring Street San Francisco, CA 94108
Phone/415-362-1990

①

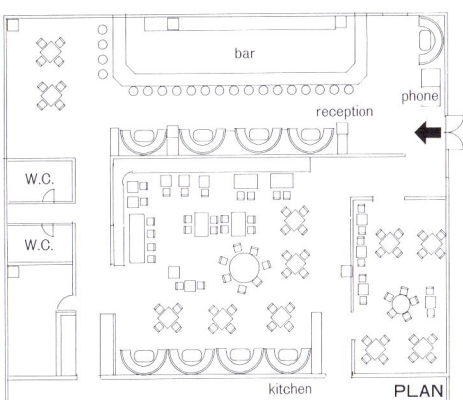

1/The reception area; with the bar at right and the dining area at left.
2/The maining dining area.
3/The facade/entrance area.

1/レセプションをみる　右がバーエリア　左がダイニングエリア
2/メインダイニングをみる
3/ファサード　エントランス廻りをみる

4/ The booth seating and table seating areas in a composed atmosphere; the bar is reflected in the mirror set on the center pillars.
5/ The private dining "Le Club Room"; also used for a party.
6/ The partition between the dining and bar areas also features the same pattern as that on the wall.
7/ The bar area; composed of counter and booth seating corners.

4/落ち着いた雰囲気のブース席とテーブル席　中央の柱のミラーにバーが写りこんでいる
5/プライベートダイニング "Le Club Room" はパーティなどにも使用される
6/ダイニングとバーエリアのパーティションにも壁面と同じパターンがデザインされている
7/バーエリア　カウンター席とブース席で構成されている

8/There is also a corner presenting a fantastic atmosphere with lighting colors.
9/The executive chef Loretta Rampone (left) and chef Ed Walsh.

8/照明の色でファンタジィな雰囲気を演出したコーナーもある
9/エグゼクティブシェフ Loretta Rampone(左)と シェフ Ed Walsh

●menu
a : ANTIPASTI MISTI / Grilled and marinated Vegetables, cured meats and cheeses.
b : GNOCCHI ALLA MARIA / Potato dumplings with lemon basil pesto.
c : PESCE DEL GIORNO / Fresh fish of the day. Grilled Salmon with Braised artichokes and Black olive caviar.

Index

restaurants in california

In alphabetical order ∗ by location/shop name

■Beverly Hills

CIMARRON ···118
    301 N. Canon Drive Beverly Hills, CA 90210
    phone/213-278-2277

LAWRY'S THE PRIME RIB ···138
    100 North La Cienega Blvd. Beverly Hills, CA 90211
    phone/310-652-2827

L'ESCOFFIER ···194
    Beverly Hilton Hotel 9876 Wilshire Blvd. Beverly Hills, CA
    phone/310-274-7777

TATOU ··200
    233 N. Beverly Drive Beverly Hills, CA 90210
    phone/310-274-9955

■Costa Mesa

EMPORIO ARMANI EXPRESS··191
    South Coast Plaza 3333 Bristol Street Costa Mesa, CA 92626
    phone/714-754-0300

IL FORNAIO CUCINA EXPRESSA ···82
    650 Anton Boulevard Costa Masa, CA
    phone/714-668-0880   fax/714-668-0440

■Danville

BLACKHAWK GRILL ···58
    3540 Blackhawk Plaza Circle Danville, CA 94506
    phone/415-736-4295

■Encino

CHA CHA CHA Encino ···24
    17499 Ventura Blvd. Encino, CA 91316
    phone/818-789-3600

TERRAZZA TOSCANA ··66
    17401 Ventura Blvd. Encino, CA 91316
    phone/818-905-1641

■Long Beach

CHA CHA CHA Long Beach ···29
    762 Pacific Avenue Long Beach, CA 90813
    phone/310-436-3900   fax/310-436-3931

アルファベット順＊地名別/店名別

L'OPERA RISTORANTE ··174
    101 Pine Avenue Long Beach, CA 90802
    phone/310-491-0066

■Los Angeles

CALIFORNIA BEACH ROCK N'SUSHI ··90
    7656 Melrose Los Angeles, CA
    phone/213-655-0123

DALE'S BISTRO ···114
    361 N. La Cienega Blvd. Los Angeles, CA
    phone/213-659-3996

LUNARIA ··142
    10351 Santa Monica Blvd. Los Angeles, CA 90025
    phone/213-282-8870

PICNIC ··197
    8771 Pico Blvd. Los Angeles, CA
    phone/310-273-1166

WATER GRILL ··166
    523 West Sixth Street Los Angeles, CA 90014
    phone/213-891-0900

■Marina Del Ray

CAFE DEL REY ···15
    4451 Admiralty Way Marina Del Ray, CA 90292
    phone/213-823-6395

■Newport Beach

HARD ROCK CAFE ···20
    451 Newport Center Drive Newport Beach, CA
    phone/714-640-8844

■Redondo Beach

BAYSIDE 240 ···50
    240 Portofino Way Rodondo Beach, CA 90277-2092
    phone/213-374-8043

■San Francisco

AQUA ···154
    252 California Street San Francisco, CA 94111
    phone/415-956-9662

CYPRESS Club ··38
    500 Jackson Street San Francisco, CA 94133
    phone/415-296-8555

ELKA ··162
    1611 Post Street San Francisco, CA 94115
    phone/415-922-7788

ETRUSCA ··74
    121 Spear Street San Francisco, CA 94105
    phone/415-777-0330

GORDON BIERSCH ··122
    2 Harrison Street San Francisco, CA 94105
    phone/415-243-8246

JOHNNY LOVE'S ··134
    1500 Broadway at Polk Street San Francisco, CA
    phone/415-931-6053

McCORMICK & KULETO'S SEAFOOD RESTAURANT ·······························70
    900 North Point Street San Francisco, CA 94109
    phone/415-929-1730

MISS PEARL'S JAM HOUSE ··110
    601 Eddy Street San Francisco, CA 94109
    Phone/415-775-5267

MODELLA RISTORANTE ··212
    7 Spring Street San Francisco, CA 94108
    phone/415-362-1990

ONE MARKET RESTAURANT ··158
    1 Market Street San Francisco, CA 94015-1572
    phone/415-777-5577

PARAGON BAR & CAFE ···130
    3251 Scott Street San Francisco, CA 94123
    phone/415-922-2456

RESTAURANT LULU ···62
    816 Folsom Street San Francisco, CA
    phone/415-495-5775

THE STINKING ROSE ··94

    325 Columbus Avenue San Francisco, CA 94133

    phone/415-781-7673

■**Santa Ana**

PLANET HOLLYWOOD ··10

    1641 West Sunflower Santa Ana, CA 92704

    phone/714-434-7828　fax/714-957-9311

■**Santa Barbara**

CAFE VALLARTA ··98

    626 E. Haley Street Santa Barbara, CA 93103

    phone/805-564-8494

MICHAEL'S WATERSIDE ··150

    50 Los Patos Way Santa Barbara, CA 93108

    phone/805-969-0307

■**Santa Monica**

BIKINI ··178

    1413 5th Street Santa Monica, CA 90401

    phone/213-395-8611　fax/213-393-9542

BORDER GRILL ··34

    1445 4th Street Santa Monica, CA 90401

    phone/213-451-1655

BROADWAY DELI ··86

    1457 3rd Street Santa Monica, CA 90401

    phone/213-451-0616

CHILLERS ··126

    1446 3rd Street Promenade Santa Monica, CA 90401

    phone/213-394-1993

I CUGINI TRATTORIA ··78

    1501 Ocean Avenue Santa Monica, CA 90401

    phone/213-451-4595　fax/213-451-9026

FAMA ··102

    1416 4th Street Santa Monica, CA 90401

    phone/213-458-6704

LUMA ···203
>　1323 Montana Avenue Santa Monica, CA 90401
>　phone/310-451-0900

OPUS RESTAURANT ··182
>　2425 West Olympic Blvd. Santa Monica, CA 90404
>　phone/310-829-2112

REMI ···106
>　1451 3rd Street Promnade Santa Monica, CA 90401
>　phone/213-393-6545

RÖCKENWAGNER ··146
>　2435 Main Street Santa Monica, CA 90405
>　phone/310-399-6504

SCHATZI ON MAIN ···46
>　3110 Main Street Santa Monica, CA 90405
>　phone/310-399-4800

■**Sherman Oaks**

POST ···208
>　14928 Ventura Blvd. Sharman Oaks, CA 91403
>　phone/818-784-4400

■**Studio City**

PINOT BISTRO ···186
>　12969 Ventura Blvd. Studio City, CA 91604
>　phone/818-990-0500

■**Venice**

NORTH BEACH BAR & GRILL ···170
>　111 Rose Avenue Venice, CA 90291
>　phone/310-399-3900

■**West Hollywood**

CAFE LA BOHEME ···42
>　8400 Santa Monica Blvd. West Hollywood, CA 90069
>　phone/213-848-2360　fax/213-848-9447

RED CAR GRILL ···54
>　8571 Santa Monica Blvd. West Hollywood, CA 90069
>　phone/213-652-9263

カリフォルニア レストラン

1993年10月25日　初版第1刷発行

定価	12,500円(本体 12,136円)
著者	斎藤　武
発行者	久世利郎
印刷・製本	凸版印刷株式会社
写植	有限会社福島写植
英文	株式会社海広社
協力	
レイアウト	ばとおく社
カバーデザイン	ウィークエンド株式会社
発行所	株式会社グラフィック社
	〒102　東京都千代田区九段北1-9-12
	電話03-3263-4318　振替・東京3-114345

本書を無断で複写(コピー)することは 著作権法上認められている場合を除き 禁じられています。
落丁・乱丁はお取り替え致します。

ISBN4-7661-0748-9 C2052 P12500E